PLACES OF GRACE

My Visits to Shrines, Chapels, Graves, and Monasteries and the Graces I Received

FATHER EDWARD LOONEY

With a foreword by Alexis Walkenstein

Places of Grace -
My Visits to Shrines, Chapels, Graves, and Monasteries
and the Graces I Received

2024 First Printing

ISBN: 979-8-9884033-3-3

Library of Congress Cataloging-in-Publication Data

Looney, Father Edward
Places of Grace -
My Visits to Shrines, Chapels, Graves, and Monasteries and the Graces I Received /
Father Edward Looney

ISBN: 979-8-9884033-3-3

Published by Bon Secours Books
www.edwardlooney.com
Printed in the United States *of* America

I have traveled to places near and far, not only by myself, but at times with groups, or individuals. To all who have been my companion, I thank you for sharing in these lessons of the spiritual life, and the graces I received from our Lord.

To Our Lord and Our Lady, the Mediatrix, and all the saints, and someday saints, who have aided me by their intercession and inspired me by their lives.

CONTENTS

FOREWORD

"Places of Grace" is more than just a guidebook; it's a roadmap for the soul, leading us to the sacred sites that have shaped the landscape of Catholic faith and devotion. Authored by Father Edward Looney, this meticulously curated collection invites us on a profound pilgrimage through shrines, chapels, graves, and monasteries, each bearing witness to the divine presence and the transformative power of grace.

As a fellow pilgrim on the journey of faith, I found myself illuminated by the pages of this book. Having personally visited many of these holy sites and with others still on my horizon, I recognize the profound impact each encounter has had on my spiritual journey. From the bustling streets of Denver during World Youth Day to the tranquil sanctuaries nestled in the heart of Europe, I've come to understand the spiritual significance of pilgrimage and the "grace of the place" it offers.

Father Looney's exploration of these sacred destinations is a testament to the enduring tradition of pilgrimage within the Catholic Church. With eloquence and insight, he unveils the hidden treasures of shrines, the mysteries of apparition sites, the sanctity of churches and chapels, and the hallowed ground of resting places for saints and blesseds. Through his words, we are reminded that pilgrimage is not merely an act of physical travel, but a journey of faith and action—a deliberate step towards encountering the divine.

In our fast-paced world, it's easy to overlook the significance of sacred spaces and the spiritual riches they hold. Yet, as Father Looney reminds us, it is through pilgrimage that we open ourselves to the abundance of God's grace, ready to receive the blessings that await us in these hallowed grounds. Each site becomes a portal to deeper communion with the divine, a place where prayer and presence intersect, igniting the flame of faith within our hearts.

I believe this book has the power to ignite a renewal of the pilgrimage mindset within the young Church. It beckons us to emulate the footsteps of our forebears, to set out with courage and conviction, and to expect powerful encounters with God and His saints along the way. Through the pages of "Places of Grace," may we rediscover the timeless tradition of pilgrimage and embark on a journey that leads us ever closer to the heart of our faith.

Yours in pilgrimage and prayer,

Alexis Walkenstein
writer, speaker, publicist and producer

INTRODUCTION

I am a pilgrim. You are a pilgrim. We are all pilgrims on earth journeying to the Kingdom of Heaven. The notion of pilgrimage is quite ancient in Christianity as early believers visited places of importance in the life of Jesus in the Holy Land. The Venerable Maria of Agreda in The Mystical City of God wrote about Mary visiting those places herself and in the years that after, believers like Egeria relate their accounts of pilgrimage to the Holy Land. Other notable works about pilgrimage include The Way of the Pilgrim and Canterbury Tales.

As a believer, I've made pilgrimages to many holy sites, beginning as a teenager, when I first visited two Marian apparition sites, one in Europe and the other in Wisconsin. I journeyed to Canada for the International Eucharistic Congress in Quebec in 2008 and was able to see many shrines along the way. In my life as a priest and speaker, I have been privileged to visit many other holy sites. The Holy Land is a very special place and the graces of the Holy Land would be better treated in a different book, as such, I will not mention my visits to the holy sites related to Jesus and Mary.

I've been blessed to travel throughout the United States, Canada, Mexico, and Europe and pray at graves, shrines, and chapels. When I have visited those holy places, I have at times prayed for a very specific grace, sometimes making the pilgrimage for that intention. Other times, I have paused in prayer thinking of what is most pressing in my life and imploring heavenly intercession and assistance. I have prayed for graces for myself or thought of people in my life who were desperately in need of prayer. A visit to a shrine is a statement of trust and belief in the efficacy of visiting a holy place. As one shrine rector in Belgium once told me, "People never forget the address of Our Lady." What he meant was that no matter a person's practice of faith, they would seek out Our Lady, ask her prayers, and light votive candles. They would recall their past experiences of faith and allow them to inform their reaction in the present.

I have had profound experiences at these shrines and have received many graces. The purpose of this book is to share places that have been significant in my spiritual life and places of pilgrimage. I like filming these shrines and producing short travel voice over videos about the shrines. These are released in a series I call "Fr. Edward Visits." Most people will not be able to see the many places that I have, either because of lack of resources, time, or interest. As I visit these places, I love sharing about them and raising awareness about them. Sometimes they are the best kept secrets in an area. Whenever I am visiting an area, I will search out Catholic sites of devotion. A visit to Nashville had me googling, "Catholic shrines in Tennessee," and I went out of my way to visit one, which unfortunately, I was not able to identify a specific grace to write about in this book.

This book is not meant to be a comprehensive guide to all the places that I have visited. I have been selective and will feature places that have made a deep impression on my heart and soul. I also need to limit how many places I selected, there are so many to choose and more visits to be made that there could be a second volume. As I name the grace I received at a specific shrine, chapel, or grave, I am not suggesting that is the only grace for which a person can pray. It was the grace that I received and now share with you the reader. Shrines, chapels, and graves are holy places of prayer, remembrance, and grace. I hope and pray as you make pilgrimages throughout your life, you will experience profound moments at such places like I have.

Father Edward Looney
February 11, 2024
Feast of Our Lady of Lourdes

ONE

MARIAN APPARITION SHRINES

The Grace of Saying Yes

The National Shrine of Our Lady of Champion

(formerly Our Lady of Good Help)

Champion, Wisconsin

I first learned of the National Shrine of Our Lady of Champion, once known as the Shrine of Our Lady of Good Help, or to locals, "The Chapel," when I was in eighth grade. My home parish was planning a bus trip to the shrine, St. Norbert Abbey, and the Carmelite monastery in the diocese. I guess my grandma wanted to go on the trip and since she was my primary caregiver during the day, I was a pilgrim on the bus that day. I recall serving at the Mass that day and at one time there was photographic evidence of it, but that picture has been lost for years. I remember serving because it was the first time I ever wore a cassock and surplice instead of an alb when serving Mass. My next visit to the Champion shrine would not be until I was sixteen years old, with a newly minted driver's license, for the feast of the Assumption of Mary. I had visited Medjugorje earlier that summer, a place of alleged apparitions of Mary. When I read about the special Mass on August 15 at Wisconsin's Marian apparition site, I wanted to attend.

I'm pretty sure when I visited as an eighth grader, I didn't grasp the fact it was believed that the Queen of Heaven had appeared at the shrine. After my pilgrimage abroad in 2005, I had a better understanding of that reality and what it meant. For Catholics who live in the Diocese of Green Bay, or Wisconsin, or even the Midwest, it is exceptional to have a shrine so close. How special it is to be able to pray at a place where Mary appeared and where many have claimed miracles have taken place. When I served as pastor of two parishes near by the Shrine, it was surprising to me that a lot of locals had never visited. I took one gentleman there during a difficult situation he was facing. He asked, "I can visit this place anytime?" He's been back since.

Mary appeared in 1859 to a Belgian immigrant named Adele Brise who was 28 years old. She was an adult, unlike the children of Fatima or the seer of Lourdes. Growing up in Belgium, Adele had been a devout child and on the occasion of her First Communion, resolved with a few other friends to enter a religious community and to work in the foreign missions. As the events of her life unfolded, that did not transpire. She was troubled by her parent's immigration to America and sought the counsel of the local priest who told her to go with them and if she was to become a sister, it would happen in America. It would be four years later when the Blessed Mother appeared and entrusted to Adele a special mission and plan for her life.

The apparitions took place in autumn, during the early days of October. They numbered three, but the Blessed Mother only spoke once. Adele was walking to the local grist mill when Mary appeared the first time. The woman said nothing and quickly vanished. Adele went home and related the story to her family. They believed the visitor to be a soul in Purgatory. On the following Sunday, October 9, Adele, her sister, and a friend were walking to the local church for Sunday Mass. Along the same trail and between two trees, a maple and a hemlock, the Blessed Virgin appeared a second time, again saying nothing. Not knowing what to make of this, Adele asked the parish priest what she should do. He advised her if the woman returned to ask her, "In God's name who are you and what do you want of me?"

That is precisely what Adele did when Mary returned for the third and final time. Her answer to that initial question was, "I am the Queen of Heaven who prays for the conversion of sinners, and I wish you to do the same." She went on to request Adele offer Holy Communion at Mass for the conversion of sinners and to make a general confession. Mary asked Adele why she was idle while her companions worked in the vineyard of the Lord. Then Mary instructed Adele to gather the children and teach them what they needed to know for salvation, how to make the sign of the cross, how to approach the sacraments, and their catechism. In her departing words, Mary told Adele, "Go and fear nothing for I will help you." It's a pretty simple apparition and message. But one that Adele responded to immediately. She went from home to home and instructed people's children. Eventually she would begin a third order of women religious and build a school. Mary asked Adele to do something, she said yes, and she did it.

The Shrine of Our Lady of Champion became a place where I prayed while discerning a vocation to the priesthood. I was a student at St. Norbert College and would often go there on Sundays for a Holy Hour they offered. It helped that the Green Bay Packers were not doing well that season and made it easier to give up Sunday football for prayer. I also served Mass at the shrine on occasion. At the time I was deciding to return to the seminary for the diocese, I was also discerning whether to join a religious community. I was pretty far along in the process, but one day at Mass when I was serving, the Responsorial Psalm was "Lord, this is the people that longs to see your face." As we repeated those words, I looked out at the people. I knew many of them because the apparitions had not yet been catapulted into a national or international spotlight with their approval. In my heart I believed the Lord was telling me, "This is the people that longs to see your face." It was a pivotal moment in my discernment as I decided to pursue entering the seminary for the diocese instead of entering the novitiate for a religious order. I realized there was a greater need at home for priests. The order I was interested in had many seminarians. Green Bay did not. In that moment, I said yes to how the Lord was speaking to me at that Marian apparition site during the celebration of Mass.

When it comes to vocation, Mary is often held up as an example because of her fiat or her yes to God. She told the angel, "Let it be done unto me." When discerning a vocation, Mary's example of saying yes to God's will inspires us to render our own fiat. The shrine in Champion has become a place where I renew my yes to the Lord as I often avail myself of the sacrament of Reconciliation there. When I have sinned and said no to the Lord's ways, by confessing my sins, I renew my yes and say, Lord, I want to do better. I will do better. I will be your disciple. For the pilgrim who visits the shrine in Champion, I'd encourage you to notice how God is nudging your heart. Mary prays for the conversion of sinners. And she's praying for you. Maybe while you are there, you will say yes to living a better life as a follower and disciple of Jesus.

The Grace of Searching and Simplicity

Shrine of Our Lady of Beauraing

Beauraing, Belgium

On November 29, 1932, Mary began appearing in a Belgian town in the province of Namur named Beauraing. There were children from two families, the Degeimbre and Voisin children. My fascination with Beauraing began because of Adele Brise and the Champion apparition. Adele was a Belgian immigrant. She died in the century before the Beauraing apparition, but given her Belgian heritage, I wanted to learn about Beauraing and Banneux, Banneux is an apparition in Belgium that followed on the heels of the Beauraing apparition in 1933. I was initially drawn to the simplicity of the messages Mary spoke to the children. She exhorted them to pray, pray very much, pray always. She told them to always be good. She promised, "I will convert sinners." Simple messages, but profound reminders.

When I was in Belgium, I intended to visit Beauraing. This was 2014, and I did not yet have a smart phone. I was traveling with Google map printouts and a GPS device. I faced a problem. I did not have the address for the Beauraing shrine. The population of the town had about 10,000 people and thinking about towns of 10,000 in the United States, I believed I could drive around the town and eventually find the place. I drove and drove. I didn't see any signs for the apparition site. I stopped at a local grocery store and in my very broken French asked the location of the woman with the coeur d'or (golden heart). The worker looked at me like I was a mad man. Belgium is a quite secularized country and I guess I had not figured out yet that not everybody would know about a Catholic Marian apparition, even in a town that small. I asked a few more people in the store, and finally a gentleman said, I will show you. I followed him and he took me right where I needed to be.

My memory of Beauraing is a bit foggy being a decade removed from my visit. I remember the small, quaint chapel where Mass was celebrated and I prayed the rosary. I happened to be visiting on the anniversary of the final apparition in January 1933. I was shocked that it wasn't a greater celebration with more solemnity. It was the middle of winter and the middle of the week. I imagined that maybe there would be a similar turnout if it was Wisconsin during that time of year. An interesting aspect of the apparition was that it took place near the railroad, almost as if Our Lady was intersecting with the busyness of one's life. Outside of the chapel was a statue of Our Lady of Beauraing, underneath the branches of a tree, because that is what Beauraing means—under the branch, and it was the spot of Mary's apparition. There also was an outdoor amphitheater area, and a larger building to accommodate large groups of pilgrims for special feast days.

After Beauraing, I visited Banneux. It was much easier to find. It was a larger campus. There were more stores on each side of the road surrounding the shrine. I wondered why Banneux was nicer. In conversations I had with clergy, they seemed to suggest that Banneux was a message of healing. People tended to gravitate more toward it. The Madonna appeared in a similar fashion as Our Lady of Lourdes and a fountain of water was involved. The shrine and apparition gave off vibes of Lourdes. I loved that the rosary has been prayed daily at the Banneux shrine in unbroken succession since the first apparitions. Yet, my heart and soul loved Beauraing. I loved its simple messages and invitation to prayer. I was aware of my need for conversion and how I wanted Our Lady to convert me as one of those sinners. That same clergyman remarked that is why people didn't feel close to Beauraing because it was more challenging. I considered it a simple challenge.

Jesus told us in the scriptures to seek and we would find. I sought the shrine and found it. I found a simple place, with a simple message, received by simple visionaries. I had the chance to meet the last living visionary while I was there. She died only a few months later. But she was simple. She didn't need recognition for being a visionary. She was simply a disciple and follower of Our Lord who heard the voice of Our Lady. She knew who she was and her purpose. I'm glad I found Our Lady of Beauraing and could be moved by the simplicity of her shrine and message.

The Grace of Participation and Remembrance

Lourdes Grottos

Various Locations

My first trip to Lourdes was in 2016 when I took a small group of family and friends to pray there for a healing of a teenager with cancer who was a part of the group. I've returned on pilgrimage there many times since. Lourdes is one of my favorite places to pray. I experience a profound peace when I visit. The Grotto of Massabielle is visited by thousands of people a day. You can sit close to the grotto on one of the benches and even with all the activity, you can ignore the sounds around you and become enraptured in the love and beauty of the Madonna of the Grotto. After the evening rosary procession around the grounds, I love to cross over the Gave River and sit right outside of St. Bernadette's Church. There are benches there and from that spot, in the distance I see the grotto and in my quiet little oasis, I continue my prayer and spend more time with Our Lady.

Before I ever went to Lourdes, the story was well known to me because of the popular film *The Song of Bernadette*, a movie I have seen dozens of times and one that never gets old. The image of Our Lady of Lourdes is also familiar to most because there are many Lourdes grottos throughout the world. Some of them are rather small and might not be a rock structure but simply a statue of Bernadette and Our Lady. Others are monumental grottos that capture the cave nature of the grotto from France. Some of the grottos are near replicas of the one in Lourdes.

One of the iconic Lourdes grottos in the United States is at the University of Notre Dame. The seminary I went to in Mundelein, Illinois has a beautiful Lourdes grotto that was renovated during my studies. San Antonio, Texas has a shrine grotto to Our Lady of Lourdes and you can find a beautiful one in Emmitsburg, Maryland. The grounds of Mother Angelica's Shrine of the Blessed Sacrament also has an amazing Lourdes grotto. Many Marian shrines, like Our Lady of Snows, have a grotto inviting people to prayer. At my first pastorate in Brussels, Wisconsin there was a grotto of Our Lady of Lourdes and St. Bernadette in the parish cemetery with a unique crucifixion scene atop it. It was not quite like the others and was built out of field stones in 1935. There is another grotto of Our Lady of Lourdes that I visited while in the Detroit metro area at Assumption Grotto Parish. Like the Brussels parish, this grotto is in a cemetery too. The story of the grotto originates with Fr. Amandus Vandendriessche who visited France in 1876 and after visiting Lourdes, wanted to share that story with others through a grotto replica at his parish. The grotto was dedicated in 1881 and has been visited ever since by parishioners and pilgrims like me.

To me a Lourdes grotto replicates the reality of the grotto of Lourdes. Not everyone has the means or ability to board a plane and fly to Lourdes, France and spend days in prayer at this holy sanctuary. An ordinary parishioner can feel connected to Lourdes by praying at a grotto. For a pilgrim who has been to France, the grotto can be a place to remember the graces of their previous pilgrimage. They can recommit themselves to love of God and the Blessed Virgin. A Lourdes-style grotto is a reminder of Mary's apparition, her message, and maternal love for all of us. Seeing a grotto can draw us into spending a few moments with our heavenly mother who prays for us. And when we stop for a few moments of prayer or to pray a rosary, we participate and remember the grace of Lourdes, France.

The Grace of Encouragement

Basilica of Our Lady of the Pillar

Zaragoza, Spain

Zaragoza and the Basilica of Our Lady of the Pillar was not on my list of places to visit while I was in Spain. A travel companion of mine recommended the visit and I was glad he did. The story of the shrine was vaguely familiar to me and I knew it was especially promoted by the Marianist religious order.

The story of Our Lady of the Pillar occurred in the years following the Lord's ascension into Heaven and before Our Lady's assumption into Heaven. The apostles were commissioned by Jesus to go out to all the nations baptizing and making disciples. They dispersed and went to different regions of the world. St. James went to Spain and that is the reason why he is highly revered there through the El Camino de Santiago and the shrine in Compostela. As the legend goes, St. James became discouraged in his missionary evangelical efforts to convert people to the gospel, and he wanted to give up. Our Lady, who was given insight into the life of the apostles by God, bilocated while still alive and appeared atop a pillar in Zaragoza to converse with St. James and encourage him in his missionary works. Many consider this bilocation the first Marian apparition.

All of us can become discouraged no matter our vocation. As I knelt in the devotional area where Our Lady is honored in Zaragoza, I thought of my own discouragements over the years, and thanked Our Lady for the encouragement she often has given me in my prayer. I also prayed for priests I knew who were struggling or on the brink of despair and prayed for their renewal. The grace that Our Lady gave to St. James is the same grace she wants to give to her sons who are priests today. They might not know how to pray or whose intercession to seek, but you do, so I encourage you to pray for the priests in your life.

The Grace to Remain

The Pines in Garabandal

San Sebastian de Garabandal, Spain

I am a big fan of Marian apparitions. People who know me know that. I wrote a book for Lent, *A Lenten Journey with Mother Mary* which unpacked Mary's apparitions and helped us to listen to her voice and live her messages in practical ways. I have studied and theologically reflected on the Champion, Wisconsin apparition and am considered an English scholar on the apparition of Beauraing. I have visited a dozen or more sites of approved or purported apparitions. I never imagined that I would become a proponent of the apparition of Garabandal. I knew that it was mired in controversy even though saints like St. Padre Pio were proponents of it. To be honest, Garabandal saved my vocation to the priesthood in 2021. It was one of the two public messages of Our Lady spoke to me at a time when the church in the U.S. was rocked by scandal. Our Lady said that many bishops and priests were leading people along the road to perdition. It's a dark message but in the darkness of what was going on in the Church, it helped me to make sense of it all.

Four children were witnesses of apparitions of St. Michael and Our Lady in the little village of San Sebastian de Garabandal that took place between 1961 and1965. Two public messages were given. One of the visionaries received Holy Communion from the hand of an angel. The story of the messages, locutions, and actions of the four children confounded me. The four girls would experience callings that summoned them to the Pines. They ran through the village and moved quicker than what seemed possible. To reach the Pines, they had to ascend a mountainous terrain, but did it with little to no effort on their part. Those who witnessed it believed it to be miraculous.

I found myself in Spain to visit the city of Agreda and desired to visit Garabandal. Because it was in the immediate aftermath of COVID it was a bit more difficult to reach there. I had to change flights last minute and go to Spain through Portugal. It all worked out and I was able to spend several days in Garabandal. It was a time of prayer and retreat for me. During my stay, I visited the pines several times. Out of shape as I was at the time, I made it to the area where Our Lady appeared. The statue of Mary is attached to a tree, almost looking like a bird house. A few benches surround it, allowing the faithful who make the climb a place to sit and pray. I couldn't tell you how many hours I spent at the pines. I did not want to leave despite the cool and raining weather. Something attracted me to the Pines and I wanted to stay as long as possible. I felt a closeness to Mary atop that hill and a great peace overcame me. The only other place where I have had an experience close to Garabandal was in Lourdes, France.

Have you experienced the grace of remaining somewhere holy before? It might not be at an apparition site, but is there anything that comes close for you? It's the desire to not want something to come to an end or have to say goodbye. Maybe the best thing that could happen to you or me is if we petition God to give us the grace to remain before Him in the Blessed Sacrament. It's a grace we should ask for after confession—the grace to remain in a state of grace. This is a grace of closeness and nearness to God. I experienced it profoundly in Garabandal, but I've also received it other places too. It's a grace available to all of us. Let's ask for it.

The Grace of Mary's Presence

The Basilica of Our Lady of Guadalupe

Mexico City, Mexico

The Church celebrates with solemnity the feast of Our Lady of Guadalupe December 12 each year. Churches with a Hispanic population go all out for this feast day which commemorates the apparitions received by St. Juan Diego. The image of Our Lady of Guadalupe has become an icon for the pro-life movement because in it Our Lady is with child. It is a symbol of evangelization, because after the apparition, missionary priests baptized more than 9 million people.

The story of the apparition was recorded in what is known as the Nican Mopohua. Our Lady appeared to Juan Diego five times. Her words were so tender. They were the words of a loving mother. Just like our mothers or people who love us have special names for us, Our Lady familiarized the name of Juan Diego to my little Juan. She asked Juan, "Am I not here, I, who am your mother? Are you not under my shadow and protection? Am I not the source of your joy? Are you not in the hallow of my mantle, in the crossing of my arms?" Mary was present to Juan in the apparition. She was reminding him of that. She was his mother and she cared very much for him. She went on to request a church be built on that spot and sent Juan to the local bishop to ask for it. Juan felt unqualified for the task and didn't believe he would be taken seriously. But he asked. The bishop requested rare, out-of-season roses as a sign of the Virgin Mother's request. Mary delivered on that request. Juan collected the roses and took them to the bishop. He held them in his cloak or tilma, and when the roses dropped before the bishop, the image of Our Lady was imprinted on the tilma. Mary's presence was felt and noted by all in that room that day.

Another part of the story about Juan and Our Lady that I marvel at is that Juan Diego tried to avoid Our Lady. He knew that if he went the same way, he would see her. He did not want to be delayed, so he went a different way. His reason was noble. He wanted to visit his uncle Juan Bernadino who was ill and dying. You can't avoid Our Lady. She appeared to him and told him that his uncle was already healed. The presence of Mary was real and powerful.

The tilma is still on display today at the Basilica of Our Lady of Guadalupe in Mexico City. It has been studied intensely and defies explanation and dumbfounds people. I've read that the image of Our Lady hovers over the tilma. The tilma is a fiber fabric that should have decayed since the apparition. Juan Diego's reflection is in the eyes of the image. The stars on the tilma comprise the constellations during the time of the apparitions. The tilma confounds and fascinates its viewers.

The shrine in Mexico City is one of the most visited religious sites in the world. To see the tilma, one must step onto a moving walkway and be whisked by the tilma. This action can be repeated numerous times. As one passes by, the presence of Mary is felt—her spiritual presence as a mother for those who seek her in that place. The joy and protection of Mary is palpable. If you were to visit the shrine on December 12, you would be among a massive crowd. They gather early in the morning and sing songs to Our Lady. It is called Las Mañanitas. A child of Mary sings to her and greets her. She, whose presence is felt at the shrine. Shrines to Guadalupe are scattered throughout the country. Where I live in the Midwest, you can visit her in La Crosse, Wisconsin or Des Plaines, Illinois. In parishes with Hispanic ministries, devotion to her is present.

Our Lady of Guadalupe is a reminder to us of what devotion to Mary signifies for each of us. If we are not visiting a shrine to Our Lady of Guadalupe, but some other shrine, her words still ring true in that place. At every altar of Our Lady, every statue of Mary, every painting, she is there as our mother. For me, Guadalupe is a reminder to remember that Mary stays close to her children.

The Grace of Silence

Shrine of Our Lady of Knock

County Mayo, Ireland

Sometime during my high school years, I bought a picture that I still have in my possession nearly 20 years later. I was thrifting at the St. Vincent de Paul Store in Green Bay. Why, I don't know. Maybe in the quest for a good deal. During middle school there was a service retreat that took place in Green Bay and during one of the retreats we volunteered at the store, processing donations and putting things out on the shelves. I'm guessing that's how I became aware of the place. The desire for religious books or cheap items must have motivated my perusing the shelves. The painting I found was of Our Lady of Knock, depicting the August 21, 1879 Marian apparition in County Mayo, Ireland. The image I bought was signed in the corner by Maire Ni Chonghaile. Over the years, as I share the story of my Marian painting acquisition, it's been reported it could have belonged to a deceased priest, and that's how it ended up at St. Vinny's.

Knock was not unfamiliar to me. I was aware of the music of Daniel O'Donnell and Dana, Irish musicians who sang renditions of the song, Lady of Knock. A verse of the song always gets to me as it builds up—"and the lamb will conquer, and the woman clothed with the sun, will shine her light on everyone." This song about a Marian apparition in Ireland might be one of the first songs I ever memorized all of the lyrics. I can still belt the song out for you today upon request.

The painting captures the description of the witnesses of the apparition. Most apparitions have visionaries like St. Bernadette, the three Fatima children, or Adele Brise for example. In Knock, a large number of people saw the apparition. It was unique. It wasn't just Our Lady, but as the song recounts, "Here I stand with John the teacher, and with Joseph at your side, and I see the lamb of God on the altar glorified." Mary came with Joseph, St. John, and the lamb on the altar. Another verse of the song tells us an important fact of the apparition, "Oh, your message is unspoken." It was a silent apparition of Our Lady. In Fatima she exhorted the children to pray the rosary every day, in Champion, to Adele, to gather the children. Knock was about Our Lady remaining and abiding with the people in a time which they suffered because of penal laws (laws passed against Roman Catholics in Britain and Ireland after the Reformation that penalized the practice of the Roman Catholic religion and imposed civil disabilities on Catholics) and hardship. Mary was with them, to comfort them for a short time, along with Joseph, John, and the lamb.

As I drove from Dublin through the countryside of Ireland, I arrived at Knock. The gable wall and the parish church were under renovation at the time of my visit, so I wasn't able to see them. But the main basilica church was open. Like the painting I acquired at the thrift store, the basilica had a mural—a large, beautiful, stunning mural—that captured the presence of the heavenly visitors. There also were arches, replicating the various structures of monasteries throughout the large church, recalling the places where monks chanted and prayed before the monasteries were left in ruins. Silence was the grace of Knock. To be silent and behold the mystery. To be silent with Our Lady, St. Joseph, St. John, and the lamb. To be silent and imagine what it was like to be one of those witnesses of the apparition. And in the silence, is the grace to listen and respond to what the Lord asks and to go where the Lord leads. Every time I look at the image of Our Lady of Knock, an acquisition that I'm happy I made, I relive the grace of silence and ponder anew the marvelous presence and unspoken message of Mary.

The Grace of Mystery

Our Lady of Walsingham

Walsingham, England

Being familiar with Marian apparitions, I had heard of Our Lady of Walsingham. For example, I knew a few facts—it was in England; the image associated with it was Mary sitting on a throne with baby Jesus; the Anglican Catholic Ordinariate cathedral in Houston was dedicated to her patronage. If you were to ask me anything more about it like who the visionary was or what message Mary spoke, I would not have been able to answer.

While in England, Walsingham was on my list of places to visit. The visit was veiled in mystery. One of my theories of pilgrimages and shrines is this: a lot of pilgrims do not understand or grasp the significance of the place they are visiting. I saw it in England at Canterbury Cathedral where passersby of the spot of martyrdom for St. Thomas Beckett simply snapped their picture and moved on. They didn't pause for a moment of private prayer. I wasn't even sure if they understood the meaning behind the picture they'd just captured. I've experienced this at the shrine in Champion—people do not know the story behind the apparition or discover all the places to pray. As a pilgrim who did not know much about Walsingham, I wanted to go there and see if I could piece together the story. Did the shrine of Walsingham communicate what took place and its importance?

As I drove to Walsingham, I told my priest friend I was traveling with my initial thoughts. For example, I had heard that there were two shrines in Walsingham, one for Anglicans and one for Catholics. I believed that the two shrines were across the street from each other. They were not. My friend hinted to me about a slipper chapel. I took a shot in the dark as to what that meant. I hypothesized that Our Lady, when she visited Walsingham, left her slipper there and it had been venerated there ever since. While a cute hypothesis, it wasn't the case. When I arrived in Walsingham, a sign along the road noted something about England's Nazareth. It didn't really connect with me right away, but soon I would understand.

My first visit was to the Anglican shrine. Thanks to a pilgrim book provided by the shrine, I began to learn the story of Walsingham. The apparition dates back to 1061 when a woman named Richeldis, a widow, wanted to honor Our Lady in a special way. Our Lady appeared to Richeldis and took her spiritually to Nazareth and showed her the house of Nazareth. Richeldis was given the dimensions and instructed to build a replica in England. At that time, it wasn't possible for pilgrimages to the Holy Land. Our Lady's request to Richeldis to build the house in Walsingham allowed people to go in spirit to the Holy Land while at her house in England. For the English people, walking pilgrimages to Canterbury or Walsingham were the most popular pilgrimage routes and remain so today. Roughly a hundred years later, the Augustinian canons took charge of the holy house and built a priory. The ruins of the priory can be visited by pilgrims today. As for the slipper chapel, it became the place of Catholic devotion. It was a wayside shrine along the way to Walsingham. Pilgrims would leave their shoes (or slippers) at the chapel and make the final trek to the Holy House barefoot as a penitential act.

According to the Miracle Hunter's entry for Walsingham, the message to Richeldis was as follows: "Do all this unto my special praise and honor. And all who are in any way distressed or in need, let them seek me here in that little house you have made at Walsingham. To all that seek me there shall be given succor. And there at Walsingham in this little house shall be held in remembrance the great joy of my salutation when Saint Gabriel told me I should through humility become the mother of God's Son." Walsingham is a place where Our Lady wishes to help God's holy people who seek her there. It was a place of mystery for me given my unfamiliarity with the apparition. As a shrine, it is a spot that commemorates a mystery of our faith, namely the incarnation, that God became man and dwelt among us. As I prayed in the replica of the Holy House, I was drawn to that mysterious day of the Annunciation when Heaven greeted Earth, when an angel imparted a message to Mary, when the Holy Spirit conceived in the womb of a humble virgin the God-man. The grace of mystery surrounds a lot of what we believe as Catholics. Our life is a quest to understand that mystery, knowing that one day we will behold the reality of that mystery in the Kingdom of Heaven.

TWO

DEVOTIONAL SHRINES TO MARY

The Grace of Mary

National Basilica of the Immaculate Conception

Washington, District of Columbia

I had seen images of the National Basilica of the Immaculate Conception throughout the years on television, especially EWTN's coverage of the March for Life and the Vigil for Life Mass. If you see the image of the sanctuary, you might be startled by Jesus. He is depicted in the apse in a mightily fashion. He looks stern and strong. It could be seen as an image of Christ as judge. Thus far in my life I have had the chance to visit the National Basilica twice. Once for the March for Life and the other during a visit for the premiere of *Christmas with the Chosen* at The Museum of the Bible. During my first visit, someone in the group captured a picture of me praying in front of an image of Mary. I used the picture as a Facebook profile picture for the longest time. After that first visit, I knew that I wanted to return one day and spend even more time visiting each of the devotional Mary altars. I hoped that I could do a retreat of several days in D.C. and visit the basilica and the chapels each day. I have not yet done that, but it is on my list of things to do sometime before I die.

The basilica is dedicated to Mary under the title of the Immaculate Conception. The bishops in the United States chose Our Lady under this title as our country's patroness. Every December 8 is the solemnity of our country's patroness, to whom we are dedicated and devoted. Construction of the National Basilica began in 1920 with the blessing of the land and the laying of the cornerstone. It was completed by 1924, when the first Mass was celebrated on April 20. Popes and saints have visited the National Basilica over its one-hundred-year history.

What I love about the National Basilica is that there are approximately 80 chapels, shrines, or grottos to Our Lady. They are situated along the perimeter of the main basilica and downstairs in the crypt. These chapels and shrines represent devotion to Mary across many cultures. There is a replica of the grotto of Our Lady of Lourdes from France and there is a special chapel dedicated for Byzantine (Eastern Catholic) prayer and worship. There are shrines dedicated to a country's devotion to Mary such as Vietnam (Our Lady of La Vang), Lebanon, or Eastern European countries. In the church there is a Latin phrase that aptly describes the National Basilica, "De Mariam Nunquam Satis,"—of Mary, never enough.

While there are many Marys depicted in these devotional chapels, shrines, and alcoves, it is important to note that these are all the same Mary, that is, they depict Mary of Nazareth, the humble handmaid chosen by the Father to be the mother of our savior. These images and areas are ways that she is depicted and how people relate to her in their lives. I love going from chapel to chapel and praying in each one, learning about the Madonna, if I didn't know about that devotion. I call the grace of the National Basilica, the grace of Mary. She is the one full of grace, and she becomes the grace for the visitor as they discover her again and again and how she has interceded and intervened for us throughout history. There are many ways a person can be devoted to Our Lady. The National Basilica invites us to discover her and fall in love with her.

The Grace of Intercession

National Shrine of Our Lady of La Leche, Mission de Nombre de Dios

Saint Augustine, Florida

Persevere in the spiritual life and over time God will reveal to you your charism. I don't know why, but early in my priesthood God placed on my heart a desire to pray for couples struggling to conceive. It might have been because good friends of mine were in this situation and it became a way that I prayed for them. I remember my first visit to the Holy Land in 2014. We were there for ten weeks and spent four weeks in Bethlehem. After that much time in a village, you became familiar with how to navigate the streets. One of the churches I would visit in my free time was the Milk Grotto. At the time, I had some apprehension about the breastfeeding Madonna image, but over the weeks it grew on me, especially after I heard the stories of couples who conceived after visiting, even though modern medicine told them it was impossible. I especially was fond of the Milk Grotto because there was an order of nuns that held adoration in their chapel, and you could visit there and pray. It may have been these visits to the Milk Grotto which began my charism of intercessory prayer (in general or for those looking to conceive?).

Afterwards, I became familiar with the original Marian shrine of the United States in Saint Augustine, Florida called Our Lady of La Leche. The articles that circulated about it online featured a quaint little chapel with green foliage growing on the outside. It too had that image of the breastfeeding Madonna and child. Given my love of Mary and interest in visiting shrines, it became a bucket list item. I longed for the day that I might visit Saint Augustine. When I made an eight-day retreat in Clearwater, Florida, I looked up how far it was from Saint Augustine, it was an unreasonable distance. When I joined some friends on a trip to Orlando, the day to visit arrived. I made my intentions known that I really would like to make the four-hour round-trip drive to pray at the La Leche shrine.

The night before we left, I posted on Facebook and Twitter about my visit, the intercessory nature of the shrine for couples struggling to conceive, and an invitation to send me a couple's name so I could pray for them by name before the image of Mary. I never could have anticipated what happened. I received more than 500 names of couples to entrust to Mary's intercession. I diligently created an excel spreadsheet on my phone so no one would be forgotten or missed and I spent a good chunk of time reading those names before I prayed my rosary. This was the first of many more visits to Saint Augustine, as I would choose to take a few days of rest in the sunshine during the winter months there so that I could intentionally pray and visit the La Leche shrine.

When a person visits the La Leche Shrine, it is isn't uncommon to see families walking around the property. It makes you wonder if the family is there because they found themselves in dire straits, unable to conceive, and they prayed there, and now return to give thanks for the grace of an answered prayer. I've spoken with families during my visits who were there for that precise reason.

In my several visits since that first one, I have continued my tradition of posting on social media and praying for couples. Over the years, my social media following has only grown, and the list each time becomes longer. But I do not tire in praying for those couples and lighting a candle at the shrine. I've had several parishioners who found themselves in this situation and I have flown there specifically to pray for them. I had the privilege of baptizing two La Leche babies. I have received several grace reports over the years from couples. They write me on Facebook, Twitter, Instagram, or email me a picture from their child's baptism, telling me I prayed for that child to be born. Those messages bring a smile to my face and renew within me that charism of intercessory prayer.

It's not unusual for a shrine to become known for a particular grace which becomes the principal reason people visit there. God hears your prayers, even you are unable to visit a particular shrine. Right now, you can pray for son or daughter, granddaughter or nephew who might find themselves in a situation of infertility. You can ask Our Lady of La Leche and Our Lady of Good Delivery to pray for them, even if you cannot pray before the image of the breastfeeding Madonna. When you are able though, praying at these shrines where pilgrims have prayed before you can be powerful. Truly they are a place of grace; a place where prayers have been answered. The La Leche Shrine instilled within me the grace to intercede for other people, and if you happen to be in that area of Florida, that grace to pray for others can be yours too.

The Grace of Direction

Schoenstatt Retreat Center

Waukesha, Wisconsin

Friends of mine throughout the years have been devoted to a way of spirituality fostered by a movement called Schoenstatt. I became familiar with the image of Mother Thrice Admirable and the Latin phrase that bordered it,"Servus Maria Numquam Peribit," Servants of Mary shall never perish. My involvement with the Mariological Society of America introduced me to two sisters of the secular institute of Schoenstatt. The founder of the movement was Fr. Joseph Kentenich (1885-1968) who served as a university chaplain. One day he gathered seminarians and students together in an old, unused chapel, and together they made their covenant of love with the Blessed Mother and they asked Our Lady to come and make her home in the chapel. Today replicas of that little chapel can be found all over the world, and in the United States in Wisconsin and Texas.

Fr. Kentenich was arrested during World War II and sent to Dachau. He survived and in the years that followed Schoenstatt underwent inquiries by his diocese in Germany. A few disagreements led Kentenich to be exiled to his religious congregation's house in Milwaukee, Wisconsin. While it could be looked as a punishment, Kentenich seized the opportunity and promoted his spirituality and the movement in the United States. In Wisconsin there is a strong Schoenstatt presence in Waukesha.

During my time serving on the administrative council for the Mariological Society of America, I was passing through Waukesha, and a fellow committee member lived at the motherhouse there. We were planning our upcoming meeting, and since I was new to the board, I thought it would be good for us to talk about expectations and things we needed to do. Our meeting went well and afterward I had plans to see the latest Martin Scorsese movie, *Silence*. A nearby theater was showing it and I would have just enough time to get there. That changed when Sister asked me or maybe better put, told me, that I should pray in the chapel.

I got into my car, buckled my seat belt, backed up and now was at the driveway. If I went left, I would go to the chapel, going right would take me to the main road. My Catholic guilt got the best of me and I did what any priest would do; I went to the chapel. At that point in my life, I had a lot going on in my mind and heart. I needed some time with Jesus and Mary. It turned out to be one of the most profound experiences of prayer in my life. As I prayed in that chapel and poured out my heart, questions, and problems to the Lord and Our Lady, I sensed the following words, "Do not worry. I have a plan for you." In my heart I believed it was Our Lady who spoke those silent words to me because as a mother she knew with what I was struggling. As I left the chapel that day, I had profound peace in my soul.

We are now years removed from that prayerful experience. But I think of it often. Partly because Our Lady's words, "I have a plan for you," has come to fruition. At a moment where I was lacking personal direction, I turned in the right direction to the chapel, and there found peace and solace for the future.

The Grace of Stained Glass Windows

National Shrine of Mary, Help of Christians (Holy Hill)

Hubertus, Wisconsin

As a young boy, I recall my grandmother sharing with me about her trip to Holy Hill. If I had to guess, she probably only went there once or twice in her life. As for me, I have been there numerous times. I have friends that live around there and when I served in Oshkosh as a priest, I was a little more than an hour away and could visit frequently. I don't remember any details of her story but I know my first time to Holy Hill as a teenager for John Bosco Youth Day excited me. I didn't appreciate my first visit to Holy Hill as much as I would later in life because I was so young and didn't know what I was looking at or why it was important. Before I was ordained a deacon, I did a five-day retreat at Holy Hill to prepare for ordination. I've brought bus groups there and have gone as an individual pilgrim. I have prayed in the chapel of Our Lady, Help of Christians and have stood in line for confession. It's a shrine that holds a special place in my heart and I'm grateful I get to visit so often.

Holy Hill is known for its natural beauty and picturesque views, especially during autumn. The hill where the sanctuary would be built had been a place of prayer and devotion long before a chapel/church came to be. In the 1860s, the local pastor Fr. George Strickner and his parishioners decided to build a chapel on the top of the hill. The small chapel was finished on Good Friday of 1863 and was dedicated on May 24, 1863. Devotion to Mary, Help of Christians would not be a typical devotion of the Carmelites but in 1906, at the invitation of Archbishop Messmer, the Discalced Carmelites arrived at Holy Hill from Bavaria and established their presence at this holy site. They have been the caretakers and custodians of the National Shrine of Mary, Help of Christians since then and in 2006 the shrine was elevated to the status of a minor basilica. The upper church of the sanctuary contains a small chapel dedicated to Mary, Help of Christians containing a beautiful statue of Mary with an older child Jesus. The statue was purchased in 1876 and was carried in procession in 1878 to the then log chapel of Holy Hill. The faithful have sought the intercession of Mary, Help of Christians for many years and stories of graces obtained and miraculous intervention abound. During a pilgrimage to Holy Hill one will see for themselves the testimonials left behind by those who have prayed there before them. For the pilgrim who offers their Aves in that chapel, they do so with great confidence that Mary will provide her help for them.

Once you arrive to the upper level and enter the main church, opening the doors and seeing the sanctuary could nearly take your breath away. In the main church, I especially love the stained-glass windows that adorn the upper half of the church. There are biblical scenes, other scenes not in the Bible like the marriage of Joseph and Mary, and then some of the saints. On the lower levels there are windows with Latin phrases. Those phrases have been included in part of the Hail Mary, to modify the name of Jesus. For example, thy womb Jesus, who ascended into heaven, Holy Mary.... This is commonly known as the clausal form of the rosary and was promoted by St. Louis de Montfort. I wrote a rosary devotional developing the practice for Catholics today, published by Our Sunday Visitor, titled A Rosary Litany. I've always marveled at those windows because of their connection to the rosary. In the chapel of Our Lady, Help of Christians, stained glass windows with the words of the Hail Holy Queen adorn the space and enhance this special place of prayer with Mary.

When I first visited Holy Hill as a teenager in the subsequent years, the St. Therese Chapel on the second floor had some multicolored banal windows. As the years went by, they sought to make the chapel more beautiful with a stained-glass window renovation. The new windows would tell the life of St. Therese of Lisieux, known by Catholics as the Little Flower, based on her autobiography Story of a Soul. The windows are stunning and invite people to fall in love with the saint of the little way. A friend of mine who had visited Holy Hill and then met me for lunch was telling me all about their visit. I asked them if they saw the chapel on the second floor. They did not. This chapel is one of the best kept secrets at Holy Hill and unfortunately not frequented by pilgrims when they visit Holy Hill. That saddens me because I love it so much.

Stained-glass windows in the Church during the Middle Ages were called the poor man's Bible. Many people were not literate but the stained-glass windows telling a Bible story or the life of a saint could relay the story to someone who couldn't read. People today are impressed by beautiful stained-glass windows. They become tools that aid our prayer life. People talk about the beautiful stained-glass windows of Sainte Chapelle or Canterbury Cathedral. They are beautiful and intricate, filled with details. It might even take someone else pointing out the little details to help us appreciate them even more. When I visit Holy Hill, I spend time admiring the stained-glass windows. Every time. I have been there dozens of times and I still marvel at and take in their beauty. For me, the grace of Holy Hill is the beautiful stained-glass windows. One of them in the St. Therese shrine has Our Lady distributing roses alongside St. Therese. A beautiful window that captures the teaching of Mary as mediatrix of grace, and a fitting window communicating the special Carmelite devotion to St. Therese and devotion to Our Lady that has been present on Holy Hill since the late 1800s.

The Grace of Fulfilling a Promise

Our Lady of Prompt Succor

New Orleans, Louisiana

It was the early 1800s, and a request was made asking the French Ursuline sisters to live and work in the United States. The sister, Mother Saint Michel Gensoul, went to the bishop and requested permission. The bishop did not want to lose another sister, and told Mother that only the Pope could grant her permission. She asked Our Lady for her intercession, praying, "O most Holy Virgin Mary, if you obtain for me a prompt and favorable answer to this letter, I promise to have you honored at New Orleans under the title of Our Lady of Prompt Succor." The Pope allowed her to establish a house in the United States, and thus devotion to Our Lady of Prompt Succor took root in New Orleans.

The famous Battle of New Orleans took place in early January of 1815. As Andrew Jackson and his army fought, the residents and Ursuline sisters joined together in prayer seeking the intercession of Our Lady of Prompt Succor. After the victory, Andrew Jackson went and thanked the nuns and those who prayed. On that day, January 8, the sisters resolved that each year on that date they would chant the Te Deum to give thanks to God for the victory and Our Lady's intercession.

These two vignettes, both pertaining to Our Lady of Prompt Succor, capture an important lesson of the spiritual life: How do we give thanks to God for an answered prayer or grace received? For Mother Saint Michel she made a promise, and kept her end of the bargain. After the battle, the community made a resolution to never forget the grace received in 1815 by gathering annually for prayer.

I was familiar with the story of Our Lady of Prompt Succor because her title is thrown around online during hurricane season. People need Mary's quick aid of intercession and help. Prayers invoking Our Lady of

Prompt Succor are believed to have averted storms and lessened the havoc wreaked by them. As I learned more about the story, the promise, and her feast day, I knew I wanted to participate one day in that anniversary and prayer of thanksgiving. Archbishop Gregory Aymond celebrated the Mass the year I went there and preached. I remember it being a very powerful and meaningful homily about Our Lady and I commented to that effect afterward in the sacristy. To be a part of a long legacy of more than 200 years of fulfilling a promise was incredible. You could almost hear the people who'd come before you chanting the hymn of praise. Year after year, our voice is added to those from before, and the praise and thanks to God is received by Him.

We all have prayed to God for something. I'm betting you have also asked Our Lady or the saints to intercede for you. What do you do when you receive the grace for which you prayed? You pray someone will be in remission from cancer, and now they are. How do you give thanks to God? The Shrine of Our Lady of Prompt Succor is a reminder to give thanks to God and be faithful to the promises we have made to God. Let that be the grace you take away from that shrine and its beautiful stories of successful intercession.

The Grace of Quiet

Basilica Shrine of Mary, Queen of the Universe

Orlando, Florida

I had never been to Orlando or its attractions until 2017. As a pastor, I'm envious of the families who are able to take their families for experiences that I never had growing up in an impoverished family. I'm sure my experience of Disney World was different as a 28-year-old than if it would have been earlier in life. I'm glad I experienced it once, but I'm not rushing back for the experience.

On one of the days, my friends thought I would enjoy visiting the Basilica of Mary, Queen of the Universe in Orlando. They owned a vacation home in Orlando, and if they were in the area on holidays or Sundays they often would attend Mass at the Basilica. It became a place for them to worship and celebrate the sacraments. Its location is close to Disney and makes it a convenient place to get away from the hustle and bustle of Orlando. Like the good basilica that it is, the priests make confessions available for several hours throughout the day. My friends often will send me a picture during their visit, indicating that they are going to confession.

It's amazing what a second visit does and how you better appreciate a place when you return. I had the chance to visit a second time while in Florida, and while I remembered much of the place, I took it all in and loved the place. Going by myself allowed it to be a prayerful, non-rushed experience. All I could remember from my first visit was the large statue of Our Lady toward the front of the church. On the second visit, I went from stained glass window to stained glass window, appreciating everything that was in the window. I found the devotional area to St. Joseph and just was amazed at the beauty of it. The teenage Jesus at a work bench, facing Joseph, who is intently listening to Jesus. The statue was beautiful. It's impact on me lasting. I will re-visit the photos I took of it, and pray about it for years to come, probably the rest of my life. The image was so powerful, I stopped a third time to pray for St. Joseph's intercession.

One of the things I loved about the Basilica was that they wanted their visitors to pray. Next to many of the statues was a little sign that had a prayer to St. Joseph, or for the Pope (by St. Peter), or the Sacred Heart. The Basilica staff had the foresight to want to teach the language of prayer and encourage prayer. The statuary is beautiful and picture-worthy. But that's not all it should be, worthy of a photo opp. The statue is meant to direct our minds to God and think of Heaven. I hope the many visitors who pass through the doors take in the beauty that surrounds them and allow it to be a moment to draw closer to God.

When a person goes on vacation to Orlando for all its many attractions, it might be easy to forget about God. The convenient location of the basilica makes the spiritual accessible, not only for Sunday Mass but also for confession and personal prayer. Sometimes in life we need a little escape from what is going on around us. The Basilica Shrine offers a place of quiet to clear one's mind, to pray, and to seek the Lord where He may be found. If the grace of quiet is something you are searching for in the middle of Disney World, you know where and to whom you can run to find that quiet and peace.

The Grace to Visit

The Rosary Shrine

London, England

I have been on Twitter, or as they call it these days, X, for a good amount of time. I remember creating a Twitter account once because Amtrak was doing a giveaway and I wanted to enter. I didn't win. I didn't become active on Twitter until after I was ordained. That was probably for the better. With writing books and doing radio, it was important to have a presence on the platform. I'm proud of my Twitter following. Of all my social media platforms it is my largest. I worked at organically growing my followers. One of the first pages I followed on Twitter was the Rosary Shrine. I probably followed them because of it being about the rosary and Mary. When I would tweet about the rosary, I would tag the shrine. Sometimes they would retweet my post.

Another Twitter priest, Fr. Lawrence Lew, lived in residence at the Rosary Shrine. I followed his content too and interviewed him once on my podcast. Fr. Lawrence is a talented photographer. He would tweet photos of the Rosary Shrine. I was impressed. I never knew I'd be able to visit England. I had planned to do so in 2020 for a gathering of Marian scholars, but COVID cancelled those plans. After completing my S.T.L. thesis which focused on two protagonists, one of which being an English Cistercian abbot, I felt compelled to visit the ruins of Rievaulx Abbey. Unfortunately doing so will have to wait for another trip to England because my week-long visit was filled with other visits. I knew if, and when, I visited London, that the Rosary Shrine would be a place I wanted to visit because of the sheer fact I followed them on Twitter from the start of my account. For most people, the Rosary Shrine would not even be on their radar. It's off the beaten path and not in a popular part of London. But for me as a lover of the rosary, Marian theologian, and devotee, it was a must visit.

My priest friend and I took a train and walked a few blocks from the station. We found the church, but finding which door to enter was more difficult. After gaining entry we spent time praying in the church. I did what I thought I should do, pray the rosary at the rosary shrine. The church had many side altars which were a part of the shrine to the rosary. These altars had a stone image representing a rosary mystery. If a visitor had the time and wanted, they could pray all fifteen of the traditional rosary mysteries by visiting each side altar. I only had time for five of the mysteries. I did, however, visit each one, taking both photos and video for whatever social media sharing and content creation I would do in the future.

I looked at each mystery and was mesmerized by a few in particular. For the second joyful mystery, you have the aged Elizabeth bending her knee as an act of reverence to Jesus in the womb of Mary. It was curious to me that only Mary was depicted with Simeon at the Presentation, when we know Joseph was there too, but Joseph is in the statuary for the Finding in the Temple. The third glorious mystery only had two angels flanking the Holy Spirit and the rays. It was a new meditation for me to think of the adoration due to the third person of the Godhead. The Coronation or Queenship of Mary depicts Our Lady as Queen of the Holy Rosary surrounded by Dominican saints. She is the Queen of the Rosary and Queen of Saints.

Sometimes when you travel, the grace is simply to visit. The travel we do might be a long time coming, something we have anticipated for years and is the fulfillment of a dream. I didn't have to visit the Rosary Shrine, but it was good that I did. Would I have prayed the rosary that day? Most certainly. Was it better that I prayed at a shrine dedicated to the rosary, where so many have meditated on the mysteries and thumbed their beads? I think so. Did praying the rosary in front of the statuary of the mystery enhance my meditation? Most definitely. That is the grace of a visit. As we grace a place with our visit, we are graced in return by God who is the giver of all good gifts.

The Grace of Disappointment

National Shrine of Our Lady of the Snows

Belleville, Illinois

As a young boy, I watched for the mail to come, and would run across the street to get it. I have fond memories of mail coming to the family home from the Missionary Oblates and the National Shrine of Our Lady of the Snows. I remember they used to send little prayer cards for the annual novena. The prayer always consisted of the Marian prayer, the Memorare. I would fill out the prayer slip, and send petitions to be remembered at the Shrine of Our Lady of Snows. If I had to guess, this is the first shrine I ever became aware of in my life.

If you are driving to St. Louis along the interstate, you might decide to stop at the National Shrine of Our Lady of the Snows. There is a huge brown sign telling you to exit. I went to the shrine when I was in St. Louis visiting some seminarian friends. It was my first visit. I hate calling the grace that of disappointment, but that's how I would describe it. I've also described other shrines in a similar fashion. A former parishioner of mine wanted to visi to the St. Jude Shrine in Chicago, run by the Claretian missionaries. I said we could go but be prepared to be disappointed. There are other shrines I have visited which I had similar feelings. They didn't live up to the hype I had built up in my mind and heart. That's why I try not to do much research before arriving at a shrine. I don't want to see pictures because I don't want to discount the place before arriving.

When I think of a Marian shrine, I think there will be a main place of devotion to Our Lady. For example, if it is a shrine to Our Mother of Perpetual Help, I envision that would be a designated area where the image of Our Mother of Perpetual Help is and there would be candles available to light. When it comes to the National Shrine of Our Lady of the Snows, it's hard to pinpoint the main devotional area on the property. If I want to honor Our

Lady under this title, where do I go? There is the modern chapel built on the grounds and there might be an image there. But is that the place a person would go for devotion? There is the iconic outdoor amphitheater and large statue of Mary. Is that the place? What does devotion look like in the winter then? The grounds of the Our Lady of Snows Shrine is quite expansive. There is a Lourdes Grotto, the stations of the cross, other various devotional areas, and small chapels too with rosary mosaics. There is a lot to see, take in, and experience while at the Belleville Shrine. Many prayers can be prayed. It's just not what I had hoped for in a shrine.

The history of the shrine is quite interesting. It all began with one of the Oblates of Mary Immaculate, Fr. Paul Schulte and his mission work in the Arctic Circle. Given the location of his mission work, he fostered a personal devotion to Our Lady of the Snows. Fr. Edwin Guild helped Fr. Schulte in promoting the devotion which eventually led to a shrine being built. People were supporting the missionary work and wanted a place to pray, the Shrine of Our Lady of the Snows became the place. The story of Our Lady of the Snows is even more ancient and is the origin story behind the St. Mary Major Basilica in Rome. It is said a couple prayed where to build a church with their benefaction. A miraculous snow fell the next day in August and it was determined that was where it should be built. The story of the Belleville shrine and the Roman legend share the commonality of a name and are not otherwise connected.

While I may have been disappointed about my visit to the National Shrine of Our Lady of the Snows, I think that's a valuable lesson to learn in the spiritual life. There are going to be disappointments. Things are not always going to be as I want or would expect. In the spiritual life there are ups and downs, peaks and valleys, consolation and desolation. The shrine didn't live up to the hype of my childhood imagination, but it was a holy place, built for a holy purpose, where God was doing amazing things though the intercession of Mary. I was able to participate in that. Receiving grace and being open to it, is never a disappointment.

The Grace of Research

The Chapel of Notre Dame de Bon Secours

Montreal, Canada

As mentioned previously, the Marian apparition site in Champion was known for decades as the Shrine of Our Lady of Good Help. The visionary, Adele Brise, insisted that the early chapels be dedicated to Our Lady under this title—above the doors was inscribed "Notre Dame de Bon Secours, priez pour nous." It would be right to assume that this was a common devotion of the Belgians to Our Lady and was the devotional she grew up invoking. In France and Belgium there are a few basilicas and churches dedicated to this title.

I was always bothered by the wrongful connection of Our Lady of Good Help to Help of Christians, Help of Prompt Succor, and other good or helping titles of Mary. I knew that Notre Dame de Bon Secours was a unique devotion with its own historical origin. In my devotion to the Wisconsin apparition, I wanted to set apart and define who Our Lady of Good Help really was with the hope of preventing misassociation. I was not successful in my attempts but now the name change helps and avoids any further confusion.

My research about Notre Dame de Bon Secours took me all over the world and was funded by a grant that I received from Mundelein Seminary. I visited the basilicas and churches of the Bon Secours in Belgium, France, and Canada. I remember sitting in one of the churches in Belgium, and I was intrigued by an older gentleman who walked in from the back of church, hardly able to pick up his feet, shuffling them along. He reached the altar of Our Lady, lit a candle, said a prayer, and left. It was a simple and loyal faith that impressed me.

This research also led me to Montreal. I'll never forget the pilgrimage. As an American, I didn't know that Canadians celebrated Thanksgiving Day on a Monday in October. It just so happened that I landed over the weekend and hoped to conduct interviews and make visits early that week. My Thanksgiving Day in Canada didn't have turkey and was not celebrated with much jubilation. If anything, I was worried I wouldn't get everything done or see everything I needed to because of the holiday.

In my research process, I began studying the life of St. Marguerite Bourgeoys. She had a good biographer in Sister Patricia Simpson, whose biographies about St. Marguerite I devoured to try to determine why she built a church in Montreal to Notre Dame de Bon Secours. Personally, I could not pinpoint the reason why it was called Our Lady of Good Help except that it existed since the time of Marguerite. St. Marguerite was given a little statute that was enshrined in the chapel. In the 1800s Bishop Ignace Bourget sought to renew devotion to Notre Dame de Bon Secours, establishing a feast day and confraternity in her honor.

The Chapel of Notre Dame de Bon Secours faced the St. Lawrence Seaway, and over the years became known as the Sailors Chapel. Today, a large statue of Mary faces the waterway, and Mary guides the sailors to harbor, just as she guides us pilgrims to the heavenly homeland. A visit to the church might be overwhelming. Hanging from the ceilings are replicas of different ships, gifts from sailors to Our Lady in order to thank her for her intercession and guidance on stormy seas.

I went to Montreal to study Our Lady of Good Help. I wanted to know the history of her title and its significance. My visit was only the beginning of my lifelong study of Mary, her titles, and her good help. I have much more to read, study, and learn. What I do know is that she will extend her good help to her faithful followers, of which I hope I am accounted.

THREE

CHAPELS

The Grace of Entrustment
The Grasshopper Chapel
Cold Spring, Minnesota

There is a chapel in Cold Spring, Minnesota which is affectionately known as the Grasshopper Chapel. This chapel was the purpose of my visit to the St. Cloud area because travel author Marion Amberg highly recommended it when I interviewed her on my podcast *How They Love Mary* and I had previously read an article about it in *Catholic Digest* and was intrigued by it.

During the 1870s the farmers of Minnesota experienced horrific plagues of grasshoppers in their land and fields. The grasshoppers devastated crops and farmers were in dire straits. The first plague of grasshoppers was in 1856 and 1857 and they became a bigger problem in the 1870s. Not only did they attack the fields, but they also found their way into churches during Mass, and altar boys were tasked with protecting the altar and priest. It became so bad that Governor J.S. Pillsbury called for a day of fasting and prayer on April 26, 1877, in hopes that God would deliver his people from the grasshopper devastation. Fr. Leo Winter, OSB from St. John's Abbey arrived in Cold Springs in May of 1877 and while celebrating Mass one day became inspired to turn to Our Lady's intercession and the building of a small chapel dedicated to "Maria Hilf" or Mary's Help. He made a pledge that, when possible, every Saturday he would celebrate a Mass of thanksgiving to Our Lady if the people would be delivered. The chapel was built, and soon thereafter the grasshopper plague ceased. From that time onward, the people kept to their promise until a tornado destroyed the chapel in 1894. The chapel was rebuilt starting in 1951 and completed in 1952 during the centennial year of the Diocese of St. Cloud. Since the dogma of the Assumption of Mary had just been declared in 1950, the chapel was dedicated to this mystery of Mary's life.

When I happened to visit the Assumption Chapel in Cold Springs, I was enrolled as a S.T.L. student through the University of St. Mary of the Lake (Mundelein Seminary). An S.T.L. is an ecclesiastical degree meaning Licentiate of Sacred Theology. I had begun the program in 2014, but due to pastoral work, was not able to resume until the summers of 2018 and 2019. And then in 2020, a pandemic halted my summer studies. The topic I had selected many years earlier to write about was on the Assumption, and even more specifically the sermons of two Cistercian monks, St. Bernard of Clairvaux and St. Aelred of Rievaulx. To be honest, my enthusiasm for the topic dissipated after 2014 and by the time I was ready to write, I wished I could have abandoned the topic in favor of something different, but I had done a lot of leg work researching, so it would be much easier to write on this topic than chose a new one. While I was at the Assumption Chapel, mindful of my thesis topic, I prayed the Assumption rosary decade and asked Our Lady's help (ironically Maria hilf) in completing my thesis for the glory of God and my Marian studies. It was a simple entrustment of a task at hand made at a place significant to my topic. When I finished the thesis, I immediately recalled that I asked for that grace at Cold Spring and knew that I wanted to make a return visit in thanksgiving. It's a long drive (six-plus hours) to say thank you to Our Lady, but it seems like the right thing to do spiritually.

You can entrust something special in your own life to Jesus, Mary, or the saints. It could be at a nearby shrine, or it could be at your local church in a devotional area where there is a statue. When we have important tasks or a significant life event, turning to God or the intercession of the saints is appropriate. It's what I did, and I hope my act of entrustment will inspire you. I never would have finished my thesis if it was not for my love of Our Lady, her prayers and help, and the encouragement of several people in my life. With Mary's help, I was successful, and for this I am grateful for the grace.

The Grace of Someone Else's Faith

Belgian Roadside Chapels

Northeastern Wisconsin

My first pastorate as a priest was in a rural setting in the original Belgian settlement area of Wisconsin. Back in the 1850s, Belgians immigrated to the United States in great droves and began settling in the peninsula of Wisconsin. One famous immigrant was the Marian visionary Adele Brise. During my years of seminary, I drove through the peninsula region of Wisconsin to northern Door County where I would board a boat and voyage to a retreat center on an island. On one of those trips, our seminarian cohort was tasked with visiting several small roadside chapels as part of a scavenger hunt. I'm not sure how many my group visited. My many visits to the Champion apparition site also afforded me the opportunity to see a chapel, though for many years it was locked, until a clear plexiglass door was installed so pilgrims could see inside. The chapels were cute and offered a unique experience of devotion to passersby.

As I settled into life in Door and Kewaunee County among the Belgian people, I took notice of these roadside chapels. It was hard not to. I oversaw four of them, two on church properties, and two in cemeteries. I would drive by chapels all the time as I traveled through the countryside. I made it my aim to visit as many as I could. A brochure put out by the Belgian Heritage Center helped with that. Loving expressions of devotion, I wanted more people to know about these chapels. I wondered how they could be better promoted. Facebook came to mind. With a goal of visiting all of them, I thought, why not share my journey, and give a tour of each chapel? Thus began the Roadside Chapels of Northeast Wisconsin Facebook page. Over the 31 days, the number of followers quickly grew, and the videos received in total more than 40,000 views. People were curious about the chapels.

I learned a lot about the chapels through my visits. The stories behind some of them are remarkable. Many were built in response to an answered prayer.

A man who fell through the ice promised Our Lady a chapel if he survived. A man who had problems with his eyesight promised if it was restored, he would build a chapel to St. Odilia. A family that struggled to have children, built a chapel after they started their family. Each chapel has a story. The chapels have also provided a place of prayer for the homeowners. One man would pray his devotional prayers in his chapel until his health prevented him. Grandparents pray with their grandchildren in the chapels. Every chapel is unique and contains items important to the owners. Statues could be reminders of a pilgrimage to a shrine like St. Anne de Beaupre or a place where sacramental records of ancestors are displayed.

I have shared the stories of these chapels with audiences through a documentary I directed and hosted called Faith Along the Road. Since I began promoting the chapels through social media, chapel owners have seen an uptick in visitors. And as the Champion apparition site becomes better known, many make a visit to these chapels a part of their Northeast Wisconsin faith pilgrimage. For me, the chapels are a reminder to stop and pray. That was their purpose in Belgium, to provide an opportunity on a walk through a field or at an intersection to pray an Our Father or Hail Mary. The novelty of some of them is their patron saint. While some are lesser-known saints like St. Ghislain or St. Donat, others are more popular. One of the frequently visited chapels by many is one dedicated to St. Peregrine, known as the cancer saint. Visitors can leave the name of someone in a petition box to be remembered in prayer. During the pandemic, I began to regularly visit a chapel dedicated to St. Roch, whose intercession was invoked during the plague. It just so happened this chapel was about three miles from my house.

A visit to a roadside chapel is often a reminder of a grace someone else received. It is there because they prayed, received an answer, and out of gratitude they built a chapel as a tribute to Jesus, Mary, or the saint. There's something special about praying in a place that meant so much to someone else. The grace of the roadside chapels inspires deeper faith and trust and prompts us to respond to what God has done in our own life.

The Grace of Nature

St. Mary's of the Oak Chapel

Indian Lake County Park, Cross Plains, Wisconsin

At Indian Lake County Park outside of Madison stands a small votive chapel. It reminded me of the roadside chapels found in Northeastern Wisconsin. As I think back to the chapel, I don't know how I first learned about it. It could have been from a frequent visitor who posts about it on X (formerly Twitter). Or it could have been someone mentioned it to me in passing. All you must do is tell me about something and I'll add it to a list and seek it out. Or if you post about it, I'll screenshot it and put it in a folder labeled "Places to Visit." According to my photo gallery on my iPhone, my first visit to St. Mary's of the Oak was in October 2020. I remember aspects of it. As I documented my trip, I had to make sure to tell people that I was social distancing, wearing a mask, and taking necessary precautions, lest I be shunned. I also was trying not to contract the virus at the time as I continued the limited ministry we were permitted to carry out. I remember making this a day trip and I visited two other nearby sites of interest, St. Anne's Chapel and Our Lady of the Fields in Plain, Wisconsin.

After I pulled into the county park, I wandered around trying to figure out where in God's creation this chapel would be located. I found a sign that told the history of the chapel. The chapel was built in 1857 by John Endres in fulfillment of a promise he made to God for his family's protection from the diphtheria epidemic. A few men hauled the stone to the hilltop for the chapel with an ox team. When Indian Lake County Park was formed, the family asked for the chapel to remain there, and so it did. A private group now oversees the maintenance and care of the chapel. While the sign was there the first time I visited, I noticed during subsequent visits that it is no longer there. I wondered if it was being refurbished or if it had fallen victim to being a religious sign at a secular county park. I noticed that where it once stood, new landscaping had been placed.

The chapel was located at the top of a hill. Looking at the sign, there were steps which one could take to the chapel. For a person who was not in the best of shape, I admit I was winded. But the view from the top was worth it, and if nothing else it was a reminder that I needed to take health and wellness more seriously, which I'm working on. The view was stunning, striking, breathtaking, or whatever adjective you might use. The panoramic view revealed all the trees and the lake which the park was built on. The chapel was something you would expect for a votive chapel. It was small. Only a few people could stand inside it at one time. At the front end was an altar holding a beautiful statue of Our Lady. On the walls were different framed images and at the back of the chapel was a logbook to record the number of visitors. Outside, nearby the chapel, were different signs with information relevant to the chapel's history and purpose.

In the beauty of nature, at the top of a hill, stands this chapel, reminding people of all faiths of the power of God, and for Catholics, it offers a place of devotion to Our Lady and perhaps to pray the forgotten Hail Mary of their youth. Any person who might happen upon the chapel in the middle of nature will find grace. Indian Lake County Park offers visitors an opportunity to hike and be in God's creation. Sometimes, this is a grace in itself, needing to take a walk to clear one's mind. This place is a reminder that we can all encounter God in nature.

FOUR

SAINT SHRINES & OTHER HOLY SITES

The Grace of the Mass

Fr. Claude Allouez Mass Site

Oconto, Wisconsin

I grew up in Oconto, a small city thirty miles north of Green Bay. If you know your Wisconsin history, it is about twenty minutes from Peshtigo, a town known because of a fire that devastated the town on October 8, 1871, the same day as the Great Chicago Fire. My family lived on the old highway in town which passed the Oconto River. I could ride my bike from my house to the Chinese buffet a mile down the road. Across the street from the restaurant stood an old wooden cross and an historical marker sign. Why? In early December of 1667, on the banks of the Oconto River, the Jesuit missionary Fr. Claude Allouez celebrated the first Mass for the Copper Culture Indians in what would become the Diocese of Green Bay. Fr. Allouez would relocate and continue his mission down the waterway in De Pere.

I recall looking at one of the historical books related to my home parish; the pastor was pictured coming down the Oconto River in a canoe in a re-enactment of Allouez's arrival. As a youngster turned teenager then young adult and ultimately a man studying for the priesthood, I always marveled at the cross. I stopped there often. I would close my eyes and imagine what the missionary efforts of Allouez would have looked like. What he would have preached or taught occupied my mind. I imagined Allouez celebrating Mass facing the east and introducing the natives to the Mass. What did his altar look like? Where did he acquire the elements for the Mass such as bread and wine?

I can only imagine the special grace the city of Oconto experienced on that day in 1667, and in the subsequent Masses that were celebrated by Allouez, and by the eventual pastors who would establish St. Joseph and St. Peter's Catholic Church, two churches serving the needs of different ethnic communities. The Mass Allouez celebrated opened Heaven and brought the presence of Christ into the community. With every Mass celebrated at a parish, God is pouring out his grace to all who attend. I have heard bishops remark that when a parish ceases to exist in a community, the quality of life decreases and there is more violence, crime, and sin. The Mass is efficacious. Each week, a parish offers a Mass intention for the living and deceased members of its community. It is a constant prayer for the local church, past and present.

The presence of the cross along the old highway was a reminder to me and the community of what happened there hundreds of years earlier. It taught me the importance of that first Mass and, for that matter, the importance of every Mass. The efforts of early missionaries like Allouez, Marquette, and the North American Martyrs reminds us of the grace of the holy Mass, and that men were willing to sacrifice everything, and leave behind family to celebrate the Mass in foreign lands. If they were willing to risk everything, then we need to pray for the grace to appreciate the Mass and be more disposed to the graces the Mass offers us.

The Grace of Gift Giving

St. Anne de Beaupre

Quebec, Canada

The parish I grew up in had a St. Anne Society. It was the equivalent to other parish's Altar Society, Ladies Sodality, or Christian Mothers organizations. They were a group of women who gathered to pray, take care of the church, and fundraise. Since I served daily Mass during the summers in my childhood, I began to learn the liturgical calendar. The feast of Saints Joachim and Anne, the parents of Mary and grandparents of Jesus, was commemorated on July 26. Around the feast day, the St. Anne's society would have a Mass intention for the living and deceased members of their society and many of them would attend that 8 a.m. Mass.

During a pilgrimage to Canada in 2008, I had the opportunity to visit St. Anne de Beaupre Shrine. While I do not remember much about that pilgrimage experience due to my youth, what I do remember is that it was such a beautiful place. It was stunning. And when I returned to visit in 2014, I was just as astonished as I was years earlier.

Growing up, I lived with my mother and grandmother. I was very close to my grandma, and in many ways, I attribute my priestly vocation to the role she played in my faith life when I was young. Whenever I visited holy sites, I would always purchase a gift for my grandmother. Since I was at the Shrine of Saint Anne, I decided to get her a rosary, since, after all, Saint Anne is the patroness of grandmothers.

Upon my return from Canada, I began work at a Catholic summer camp. That summer there were two counselors who were not from Wisconsin. One weekend several of the counselors made a decision to visit the National Shrine of Mary, Help of Christians, also known as Holy Hill in Hubertus, Wisconsin. The church had received the designation as a minor basilica and had a Carmelite monastery attached to it. The weekend of our pilgrimage fell on the memorial of Saints Joachim and Anne. Since we were at the National Shrine on that occasion, I thought it would be appropriate to get my grandmother a gift for what I called "Catholic Grandmother's Day." In the gift store, I found a little novena booklet to Saint Anne and decided it was the right gift to give my grandmother.

I am not sure if my grandmother ever used the Saint Anne Rosary or the novena booklet I gave her. Regardless, I found the presence of Saint Anne extraordinarily powerful in my life when my grandmother passed away in July of 2010. Her death was extremely difficult for me, and while it was expected, it was at the same time unexpected. Her health had been deteriorating since I entered college and she had been in and out of the hospital and nursing home for various reasons. When my grandmother was dying, I was studying in Omaha, Nebraska as part of the Institute for Priestly Formation at Creighton University. After having received a call from my mother, I was able to get on the next flight from Omaha to Milwaukee in order to be at my grandmother's bedside when she passed.

As is the custom, my family had to find a rosary to place in the hand of their beloved dead. When I was searching through the rosaries she had, for she had many, I found the rosary from Saint Anne De Beaupre, and I knew that it was the perfect rosary to use, given the meaning it had to me and the role of Saint Anne in the life of Jesus.

After her funeral, I remained in Wisconsin for a few days. The Saint Anne rosary was not the end of Saint Anne's presence in my life following my grandmother's death. The day that I was leaving to return to Omaha, I attended Mass at my home parish. On that day, the Saint Anne's Society had their annual Mass intention. Following the liturgy, the members renewed their consecration to Saint Anne. I could not help but think that only a few days after my grandmother's funeral, I was being reminded of Saint Anne.

When I returned to Omaha, life resumed as it was before. During the summer, seminarians were given one ministry assignment, whether it was being a lector or a server. What day was I selected to exercise my ministry assignment of serving? None other than the memorial of Saints Joachim and Anne.

After my grandmother's passing, I developed a devotion to Saint Anne, the same devotion that I tried to cultivate in her life by those small gifts. I noticed more Saint Anne statues with the child Mary in churches than I ever had before. Whenever I see a statue of St. Anne, it always is a reminder to pray for my grandmother and recall the many fond memories I have of her. When I visited St. Anne de Beaupre in 2014, I was able to have the gift of a Mass celebrated for her soul. The gift of a rosary while she was alive and the gift of a Mass intention for her eternal repose. Those gifts I gave my grandmother in 2008 have become Saint Anne's gifts to me, a special grace from a woman I loved dearly.

The Grace of Passing By

The National Shrine of St. Philomena

Briggsville, Wisconsin

A few friends and I once talked about visiting the National Shrine of St. Philomena in Briggsville, Wisconsin. It was probably about two-and-a-half-hour drive. We never made the pilgrimage together. My memory of what the place would promise was skewed as I thought it was more of an expansive property. To my surprise during my first visit, I discovered a simple outdoor grotto to St. Philomena at the parish church of St. Mary, Help of Christians. Fr. I.C. Wiltzius dedicated the Briggsville shrine in 1947 after having obtained a relic of St. Philomena ten years earlier. The simple outdoor grotto was to bear resemblance to the dungeon where this young saint suffered in defending and preserving her virginity.

I became familiar with the story of St. Philomena through a talk distributed by Dr. Mark Miravalle. I was mesmerized by this little saint who seemed to be a wonderful intercessor for so many, including saints like St. John Vianney and St. Pius X. The historical story of St. Philomena is met with skepticism because being a virgin-martyr. Not much is known about her, except that the relics of this saint were discovered in the Catacombs of Priscilla in Rome, and as soon as they were transferred, miracles began to be attributed to her intercession. There are several books available if a person wishes to familiarize themselves with the story of St. Philomena and why people ask her for help and prayers.

In the past few years, I had some friends who moved to the area of Briggsville. I made my initial visit to the shrine during my first visit to see the home they built. I've been back there a few times and each time I make a point to go out of my way and make the side journey to say some prayers at the National Shrine of St. Philomena. It's probably about twenty minutes out of the way but it seems like the right thing to do. I don't have a particularly strong devotion to her but my guilty conscience might get the best of me if I skipped the visit. The more I thought about it, I wondered if this was a grace. After having driven a few hours, and being about half an hour away from my friend's house, I have the opportunity to stop and pray. I might pray my breviary which I promised to pray daily at ordination. Or I'll pray the rosary, because there is a connection of Marian devotion to St. Philomena. I usually will pray the litany of St. Philomena and whatever petition is on my mind I'll ask her to pray for at that moment.

I call this the grace of passing by. As I pass by the area where the shrine is, I make a point to stop, but as I do so, I know that God wants to give me grace. That, as I call out to Him in prayer and with the assistance of St. Philomena, God wishes to give me something. I might not know what, but by the very fact that I stop by, I know there will be a gift given to me from God on high. Whether I'll know what that grace is in the moment or I'll have to wait until the Lord makes it known, grace is received.

One of the things that has struck me during my visits to the St. Philomena shrine is its emptiness. I'm not sure I've ever seen another pilgrim there. I know the town of Briggsville has less than 500 residents, but it surprises me that no devout person from the town has been there any of the handful of times I've visited. As believers, we are blessed with these little oases of peace and grace. At a parish I served there was a grotto to Our Lady at the center of the cemetery. My hope and vision were to make that grotto a place of frequent visitation and constant prayer by parishioners and passersby. If I lived in a village blessed with a special spot for prayer, I would want to visit as often as I could, daily if possible, weekly at best. If you find yourself passing by a church, a statue, a shrine, or chapel, you might consider stopping, because when you do, the God who is the giver of every good gift will look upon your act of love and devotion and give you grace to help you as a disciple.

The Grace to Return

The National Shrine of Mother Cabrini

Chicago, Illinois

Sometimes you learn about a shrine from other people. They might bring it up in conversation, tell you stories of their experiences there, or recommend you make a visit. That is how I first heard about the Mother Cabrini shrine in downtown Chicago. Or maybe I should say that is how I heard about it the second time. When I was attending Mundelein Seminary, I remember hearing about the Mother Cabrini shrine. But my recollection was someone told me it wasn't that impressive and that it was basically a shrine in the basement of a hospital. I kept that in my memory and made a note that it would be difficult to visit. In the autumn of 2021, I was talking to a fellow author friend who lives near the Cabrini Shrine, and she told me how amazing it was and that I needed to visit. This friend also wanted me to interview the director of the shrine for my podcast *How They Love Mary* (now called, *Hey Everybody! It's Fr. Edward*). I thought before the interview I should visit so I could speak intelligently about the shrine.

When I made my first visit, I discovered how hard it was to find parking. But if you circle the block long enough or are a pro at parallel parking, you will be fine. If you are driving by, you might miss the Mother Cabrini Shrine, because it looks more like a hotel entrance than a Catholic shrine. But don't let that fool you. What I vaguely remember hearing seems to have had some aspects of truth. The shrine is on the first level of what used to be a hospital in Chicago.

As I walked up into the shrine church, my jaw nearly hit the floor. I was immediately impressed by the space. It communicated to me the story of Mother Cabrini. The ceiling contained murals of her life and journey from Italy to America. Mother Cabrini originally wanted to be a missionary to the East, but when she consulted with the Holy Father, she told her to go to America. She served throughout the United States. There are shrines in her honor in New York and Golden, Colorado. She died in Chicago and the museum contains a replica of the room in which she died.

The shrine itself contains a relic of an arm bone underneath the altar. As you walk around the church you will discover devotional niches and other pieces of Mother Cabrini's story. The miracles which led her to beatification and canonization are depicted in stained glass windows, like the story of baby Peter Smith. A nurse was washing the child's eyes with silver nitrate, but the concentration was much too high, and it caused his blindness. Mother Cabrini's intercession was invoked and a relic brought to the baby. The next day when the doctor examined the child, he thought he was brought the wrong baby because the child's eyes were completely normal. A miracle indeed and the baby went on to become Fr. Peter Smith.

When I visited the Mother Cabrini shrine, I admittedly didn't know too much about her. I knew that St. Francis Xavier was her patron. That she was Italian and immigrant. I could give you a ballpark time of her memorial date. I learned so much about her from the church, a tour, and the museum. And there was something attractive about her that inspired me to read her biography and learn even more. The Chicago shrine made an impression on me. Again, I was struck by the beauty of the shrine church and the spirituality the shrine exuded. I really believed they understood Mother Cabrini and communicated her life and message to me as a pilgrim.

It just so happened that a few weeks after my initial visit, the shrine was launching a holy year with a special indulgence and holy door. It meant that I had to return. My first visit with friends was a bit rushed. I wanted the second to be more prayerful so I could appreciate this American saint. I was able to do just that and found great peace during my visit. I was so deeply moved by the story of Mother Cabrini and her shrine that I have shared it with others. I returned with a busload of pilgrims from my parish so they too could participate in that special indulgence for her jubilee. And I know it will be a place I visit when I'm in the heart of Chicago. This is the grace of returning.

To go back and find the peace and comfort I previously experienced. It is knowing that I have a spiritual home and another intercessor on my behalf. When I return, I might not have specific or urgent request, but I intend to quietly ask this saintly missionary sister to pray for me and my intentions.

The Grace of Gratitude

Blessed Solanus Casey Center

Detroit, Michigan

My admiration and devotion to Blessed Solanus Casey grew out of my study of his life in anticipation of his beatification. Reading one of his many biographies made a deep impression on me and I knew how I needed the prayers of Blessed Solanus Casey. In the biography I read, I learned about Solanus Casey's hospitalization and potential need for an amputation. This fact about his life resonated with me because at the time my mother was still alive and already had several toes amputated and faced the amputation of her leg. I believed he would be a holy helper for her and so daily I began asking Father Solanus to petition God that my mother would never have to have her leg amputated.

As I kept reading the biography, I learned even more about Blessed Solanus. As the porter of the friary in Detroit, he would receive many people who would ask for his prayers and seek his counsel and advice. One of the practices Blessed Solanus encouraged was having people read the Mystical City of God, a multi-volume biography of Mary written by the Spanish mystic Venerable Maria of Agreda. He would give them a copy of the work and encourage its daily reading, to have faith in God, and all would work out. Some people would return to Blessed Solanus and ask him why the person they brought to his attention was not getting any better. Inevitably, the person had not read the Mystical City of God and once they started, they often would receive the grace they were requesting. I don't know why reading that work was so efficacious or why Blessed Solanus believed in it so much, but it seemed to work for so many who came to him.

Mindful of my mother's situation, I began not only asking Blessed Solanus to pray for her but each night I would say my prayer asking his intercession and then read a page or two from the Mystical City of God. My mother passed away a few months after I began that devotion, but she never had her leg amputated, and for that reason alone, I counted it as an answered prayer through Blessed Solanus. I placed a Solanus Casey relic badge in her casket. I didn't stop asking Solanus to help me then. Because with her death, I needed to sell her home. For a few months I tried to sell it independently. I had no luck. I began asking Solanus to be my relator and help me sell the home; I know St. Joseph usually helps with that, but I was keeping with the devotion already established. I professionally listed it and the next day it sold. I was grateful again to Solanus Casey and how he came through for me.

Once the paperwork was finalized and I handed over the keys, I decided I needed to go to Detroit and thank Solanus at his shrine and to pray before his body. It's quite fitting where Blessed Solanus is placed at the Solanus Casey Center because he is entombed right at the entrance of the Church. He still maintains his role as a doorkeeper to this day. It was important for me to visit his tomb and to thank him for the many ways that he had interceded for me. One of the popular sayings of Blessed Solanus was to, "Thank God Ahead of Time." Not only can we thank him ahead of time but most certainly we should after a grace is received.

You might have a devotion to a saint and ask for their prayers. This devotion might lead you one day to visit where they are buried or to honor them at their shrine. If that isn't possible, as an act of gratitude, you might want to acquire a statue of the saint for your home so you may be reminded always of their recourse in your life. Or possibly you will happen upon an image or statue of the saint in a church where you can continue to foster your devotion to them, not only of petition, but of gratitude too.

The Grace of Dedication

Convent of Venerable Maria of Agreda

Agreda, Spain

As I shared, Solanus Casey brought me to a point of devotion to the Mystical City of God, a 2600-plus page biography of Our Lady inspired by the mystical revelations received by Venerable Maria of Agreda. Maria became an abbess at a very young age and some of her family members joined the new community which was formed in the family's castle. The revelations that Maria received often were in her private prayer with God and Our Lady, and she was instructed to record and share those revelations.

If writing such a voluminous work was not impressive enough, Maria of Agreda bilocated from her monastery in Spain to the United States and began teaching the Jumano Indians throughout the Southwest. These bilocations are reported to have taken place in San Angelo, Texas, New Mexico, and Arizona. The natives would later receive missionaries who came to instruct them in the faith and the missionaries were surprised when the natives could articulate articles of the faith and repeat their prayers. The missionaries asked them how they learned the faith and they shared about the Lady in Blue who taught them. A painting of Sor Maria was brought to America and when they saw her image they identified her as the one. Maria of Agreda even wrote about it in her autobiography and the monastery museum has an altar cloth with Jumano images on it that Maria of Agreda brought back from one of her bilocations.

My love of Sor Maria and the growing devotion I had to her started because of Solanus, and led me to accept a speaking engagement at a Marian conference in the Diocese of San Angelo during that weekend a statue of the Lady in Blue was dedicated. One of the reasons I accepted the invitation was because I believed I owed a debt of gratitude to the role of Sor Maria in my intercessory prayer for my mother. Admittedly, what I started at the inspiration of Solanus Casey, I never brought to completion. When my mother passed away, I stopped reading daily from The Mystical City of God. The volumes collected dust and were put back on my bookshelf. I pulled them off the shelf from time to time, especially when I wanted to reference a rosary mystery and or incorporate Sor Maria's writings into a reflection.

In the 2020s several different Catholic apostolates began projects of reading certain books or devotionals in a year. It all began with Fr. Michael Schmitz and his reading of the Bible in a year with commentary. Then Fr. Joseph Roesch, MIC added his project of reading the Divine Mercy in my Soul, the diary of St. Faustina, in a year-long podcast. Crazy me wondered why not do something similar for The Mystical City of God. I texted a priest friend the idea and he never responded. Probably because he thought that was too big of a project. After consultation with TAN Books, who published the English volumes, I set out to do what seemed unreasonable and impossible. Every day I recorded a reading of seven to ten pages and then I personally edited the recording too. I'd upload and post the episode and, to my surprise, people were reading along with me. Given the very niche work that The Mystical City of God is, I was delighted when, by the end of the first year, the episodes were downloaded more than 125,000 times. People were able to share their thoughts and insights in a Facebook group. I was deeply moved by the response of the people and because of them I persevered through the reading and completed the project even though some days I wanted to give up.

I had the chance to visit the monastery in Agreda, Spain and I spoke with an English-speaking sister about Sor Maria. I was able to share that conversation as a podcast episode. Sor Maria is an incorruptible and you can pray before her body in the convent chapel. As I knelt there, I asked her to pray for all the people who were listening to the program and those who would listen in the future. The monumental work I began in sharing the audio and written reflections of The Mystical City of God took much dedication on my part. If I didn't have the strong conviction of the importance of the work, I wouldn't have started or continued. But because I wanted to make the work better known and I hope to see Sor Maria as a saint of the Church one day, I persevered with the project. You might find that you also have a major project that you want to undertake and at times it would be easy to give up. But if you have a holy intercessor who inspires the project or who you have asked to watch over and intercede, you will not give up, and remain dedicated to the task at hand. For me, it was Sor Maria, and I didn't want to let her down. With the project complete, I hope she is smiling from her place in eternity. Your dedication to whatever project you are working on may also bring delight to the heavenly courts.

The Grace of Adoration

National Shrine of St. Maximilian Kolbe (Marytown)

Libertyville, Illinois

I attended major seminary at the University of St. Mary of the Lake, known to many as Mundelein Seminary. Next door to the seminary is a national shrine dedicated to St. Maximilian Kolbe. It is known also as Marytown. Marytown was a concept of St. Maximilian Kolbe. A town that would honor Mary, the Immaculata, and Eucharistic adoration. Marytown as a Catholic institution and shrine, fulfills the vision of St. Maximilian Kolbe.

I'll never forget one time when I took someone to visit Marytown while they were visiting me at Mundelein Seminary. After we prayed and toured the little museum to St. Maximilian, on the way to the car, my friend said to me, "That place felt overly feminine." He was not referring to the friars that served the place. He meant the feel of the building. I was surprised he could pick up on it. Marytown used to be a monastery for a foundation of Benedictine Sisters from Clyde, Missouri. I'm guessing as a homage to this history, the friars kept a statue of St. Benedict and St. Scholastica near the doors of the main entrance.

I am not sure what would have graced the side walls when the Benedictine Sisters lived there, but today there are beautiful paintings depicting various Franciscan saints. One of them depicts Blessed Duns Scotus, who eloquently described and defended Mary's Immaculate Conception, paving the way for its eventual dogmatic definition in 1854. A mosaic representative of the Heavenly court adorns the sanctuary and includes a bit of local Catholic history. A large monstrance is elevated high in the main sanctuary, allowing all in the chapel to adore and pray before the Blessed Sacrament. At times the church is filled with lots of people and at other times it might be just two or three people and a friar in the choir stalls praying.

I have found myself also drawn to the stained-glass windows and have attempted capturing pictures of my favorites time and again. Off of the main chapel where adoration takes place are two separate devotional areas. One is the designated area for St. Maximilian Kolbe throughout the year, except during Christmas, when, if I'm not mistaken, the nativity scene takes over the space. Candles and other statues are placed in the area for the sake of devotion. The other chapel is devoted to Our Lady of Seven Sorrows, a meaningful devotion especially during Lent, but one that some identify with throughout the year. The seven sorrows are depicted in paintings throughout the chapel, of which, two were familiar to me because they were the same paintings that adorned the front of the church I grew up in Oconto, Wisconsin. During my summer studies for a Licentiate in Sacred Theology, I often concelebrated the daily Mass that was offered early in the morning in that chapel. I spent a lot of time praying and admiring the beauty of the Mother of Sorrows chapel.

Marytown offers a beautiful gift to people in the northern Chicago suburbs. It offers the gift of adoration. Adoring the Lord in the Blessed Sacrament is available every single day, day and night. The church is always open and available to people who need a moment with the Lord. Both as a seminarian and as a priest, Marytown was a place where I could go to pray. Sometimes it was nice to have a change of scenery and to pray before the monstrance.

Adoring the Lord in the Blessed Sacrament was instilled in me during my youth. My home parish would have weekly adoration on Fridays after daily Mass, for half an hour. Like many, I didn't know what to do during adoration, so I either prayed the rosary or read a book. We had weekly adoration on Sundays during my time at Conception Seminary. It was a part of my spiritual life. But through Marytown, I fell in love with adoration, and began to see it as a time to talk to the Lord from my heart, directly to His heart. I began to understand what a man once told St. John Vianney, "I look at Him, and He looks at me." Marytown bestowed on me the grace of adoration. I don't get to Marytown as often now that I don't live next door. But every time I return to pray, it's always a familiar environment, where I encounter the Lord in the Blessed Sacrament, speaking and listening to Him. This is the grace of adoration.

The Grace of Connection

The National Shrine of St. John Neumann

Philadelphia, Pennsylvania

I met a gentleman while I was visiting the alleged Marian apparition site in Garabandal, Spain. He joined my friend and me for dinner each night at the local hotel where he was staying. We had incredible conversations and he shared many of his experiences as a musician, and the amazing places he performed. He also relayed to me his connection to the National Shrine of St. John Neumann, a priest and bishop who served in America, but who might be an unfamiliar name to those who don't study American Catholic history. I found myself in Baltimore to deliver an address to a Legatus chapter. I had a whole day to myself before the evening talk. I looked up how far Philadelphia was from Baltimore. The answer around two hours. As a Wisconsinite, two hours one way to visit a shrine and a person I knew was reasonable. It would mean four hours round trip, but I deemed it worth it. I rented a car and headed to Philadelphia to learn the story of St. John Neumann and enjoy a lunch with my new pilgrim friend from Garabandal.

I arrived in Philadelphia from Baltimore without a problem and no traffic at all. I have traveled all over the world now, but it still amazes me that I am able to navigate large cities and the corresponding highways and byways. My greatest problem was the city streets of Philadelphia and the limited parking in the shrine lot and my uncertainty if I was going to get towed or not. I arrived at the shrine earlier than I expected, which gave me sufficient time to look around and explore the property and church. I walked around the church and took in the story of St. John Neumann as it was conveyed through the stained-glass windows. I was impressed by the mosaic of St. John Neumann which had green and gold candles in front of it. In the city of brotherly love, I didn't think the colors were for the Green Bay Packers. I digress. I marveled at the altar where the holy sacrifice of the Mass was offered. Beneath the altar was what appeared to be St. John Neumann. I quickly Googled to see if he was incorrupt. He was not. This was a wax mold meant to present his likeness. Overall, the shrine church did a marvelous job presenting the life and story of St. John Neumann. Before even visiting the adjacent museum, I felt like I knew the man.

As I walked through the museum and read the placards about his life, I felt an immediate connection to St. John Neumann. It was as if I understood him and he understood me. His quotes on the wall seemed like phrases worth repeating in my own prayers, "O my God, I have consecrated myself to You! Do with me whatever is most pleasing to You." "Dearest God, give me holiness." Every quote, every tidbit of his life, resonated with me. I knew that he had to be one of my holy patrons and intercessors. He had a great love for Mary and he promoted the forty-hours devotion. Our Catholic education system as we know it was inspired by St. John Neumann. His contributions to the Church were significant; his legacy continues today.

It was because of a connection I made while in Spain that I even found myself in Philadelphia to discover a saint with whom I shared much in common. As I continue to navigate life, I find myself looking to the example of St. John Neumann and asking him to pray for me, because I feel like he knows and understands me. For another saintly intercessor, to whom I felt a strong connection, I am thankful. I hope to return to Philadelphia soon, perhaps to take in a football game between the Philadelphia Eagles and Green Bay Packers, but most especially to draw closer to St. John Neumann.

The Grace of Miracles

The Staircase of St. Joseph

Santa Fe, New Mexico

I was supposed to lead a pilgrimage to Lourdes in 2021. Unfortunately, because of the pandemic, interest was not there for the trip and it was cancelled. I already had my priest coverage for that weekend lined up so I decided to take time away in the United States. I chose to go to New Mexico. One reason was that I wanted to visit the monastery of sisters established by Mother Mary Francis, PCC in Roswell, New Mexico. The second was because it was still the Year of St. Joseph and I wanted to visit the miraculous staircase of St. Joseph in Santa Fe.

Growing up my family loved *Unsolved Mysteries*. I remember Robert Stack's voice and the cases they explored. As an impressionable youngster, I never forgot their coverage of this staircase. The story of the staircase was also captured as a movie called The Staircase.

As the story goes, the Loreto Sisters built a new chapel. After it was built and the sisters were readying for its consecration, it was realized there was a choir loft, but no staircase to access it. Contractors told them it would not be possible to construct a staircase. The sisters turned to God in prayer, and specifically St. Joseph, who was known as a carpenter. A mysterious man, later identified as Frenchie Rochas, showed up at the conclusion of the novena and offered a plan to the sisters. It was to be a spiral staircase. The legend tells us that the man constructed the staircase and vanished without payment or thanks.

In addition to the miraculous answer to prayer, there were other miracles surrounding the staircase. The type of wood used was not from the local area but was common in the Holy Land. The staircase was held together not by nails or glue, but by wooden pegs. The physics of the staircase defied scientific explanation.

The convent of sisters for whom the staircase was built no longer pray in the church. It has become a museum. You have to pay admission to enter but some funds do go to the retirement of the sisters, if memory serves. My visit to the chapel was made in the spirit of a pilgrimage. I prayed a rosary in the church and meditated on the life of St. Joseph. I prayed in thanksgiving for the sisters who prayed in the space for decades and for a greater devotion to St. Joseph for myself and all who visited.

A person is overcome by awe when looking at the staircase and processing the story associated with it. Even greater, is that these sisters prayed to God, asking for a solution to their problem, and they received a miracle in return. If anything, the staircase reminds us to believe that our God is a God of miracles. Don't be afraid to make a big ask of God, because he just might deliver. Let the staircase and its story leave you with a sense of the miraculous.

The Grace of Being Pursued
The National Shrine of St. Elizabeth Ann Seton
Emmitsburg, Maryland

Of all the American saints and blesseds, St. Elizabeth Ann Seton is one whom I am most unfamiliar with her life and story. Even after visiting her shrine in Emmitsburg, Maryland, I still remain clueless as to much of her life. Her feast day falls each year on January 4, and I'm sure I read a little bio of her and say a little something about her at Mass. I'm willing to bet my words about her life are not profound.

I found myself at her shrine for one reason—effective marketing. I never looked up the shrine. Perhaps my cellphone knew that I was going to be in Baltimore and the algorithms began sending me their promoted posts weeks before my visit. It could be that I'm a shrine junkie and follow many shrines on social media and that put me in their marketing reach. I felt that I was being pursued by her or the shrine.

That happens from time to time. It could be with a saint. God is trying to break through to us and keeps sending the same saint through social media memes. As you see the memes, then you come across their name in a book you are reading. This might lead you to further inquiry or research about the saint. It could happen with a bible verse. Rev. Nicky Gumbel, who created the Alpha series, related a story of a recurring bible passage in his life. After a relative passed away, he doubted their eternal wellbeing. On several occasions he continued to come across a Bible verse from Romans 10:13: Whoever calls upon the name of God will be saved. And when he didn't see the Romans verse, he was directed to the only other occurrence of that phrase in scripture, Acts 2:21. He believed that God had a message for him and that this wasn't just a coincidence. This verse was meant to console him in the wake of that death.

I don't know why God led me to St. Elizabeth Ann Seton and her shrine.

I thought it was a beautiful church and I was blessed to pray before her remains interred in the Church. I don't remember what I prayed for, but probably my usual intentions in that situation or for her prayers regarding whatever I was going through at that moment. Asking the prayers of a saint of Heaven definitely never hurt anyone, and that's why I made a point to stop at her shrine when I was in the area. She was pursuing me and I'll only know why when God reveals it to me in this life or in the life to come. Pay attention and see how God is pursuing you in the spiritual life.

The Grace of Beauty

Shrine of the Most Blessed Sacrament

Hanceville, Alabama

People should not be surprised that I have a great love for the Eternal Word Television Network (EWTN). I watched EWTN growing up as a kid. I was not your normal youth. I loved their *Life on the Rock* show and I would watch the shows for older people like Mother Angelica or Fr. Benedict. I've been a guest on a number of EWTN shows throughout my priesthood, often speaking about books and experiences. I went from being a viewer to being a guest who others were watching. It was a full circle experience.

If I tuned in at the right time on a Sunday, I might happen to see exposition and benediction from the Hanceville shrine. EWTN is in Irondale. Mother Angelica founded her monastery and built a shrine to the Blessed Sacrament in Hanceville. The two are separated by an hour drive.

When you see the Shrine of the Blessed Sacrament on television, it appears to be a grand place, built to the honor and glory of God. The gold of the building stands out. On television you can see the grille which separates the sisters from the world. Just as stunning as it is on television, it's even more so in real life. It would be easy for someone to look at the Shrine of the Most Blessed Sacrament and think that typical thought, what a waste to spend on all this money on a building when it could have gone to help the poor. If I had to guess, Mother Angelica would tell you that God deserves the best and that is why she didn't spare any expense. She built a beautiful throne room for her God who reigns from the tabernacle.

When you reach Hanceville, you feel like you have arrived in Italy with the architecture that surrounds you. You have left the ordinary world and now enter a sacred space and time. One is not permitted to take photos in the main shrine out of respect for the Blessed Sacrament. The shrine is meant for prayer and not a photo opp. In the crypt of the shrine, is a lower chapel.

It is unequaled in its beauty. The back wall of the crypt is the mausoleum for the sisters. Mother Angelica is entombed there, and a pilgrim visitor can spend time praying before her tomb. The graves of other nun, including her mother who entered the monastery, are present, reminding us that they left the world to pray to God and by their death point us to the eternal realities that await us.

There is so much to take in on the grounds. I walked the outdoor Stations of the Eucharist that Mother Angelica crafted. It is a shrine to the Blessed Sacrament. Mother Angelica wanted the visitor to walk away knowing and believing that Jesus is present body, blood, soul, and divinity in the Holy Eucharist, and that this reality was foreshadowed in the Old Testament, long before Jesus instituted the sacrament on the night of the Last Supper. The Lourdes Grotto on the property is a near replica of the one in Lourdes, France. When I return, I know I'll be spending a considerable amount of time praying there with Our Lady.

Everything in Hanceville is about the grace of beauty. It is the beauty of being Catholic and professing what we believe. It is the beauty of our faith, teachings, and traditions. It is the beauty of a life consecrated to God lived out by the nuns who reside within the cloister of the monastery. A visit to Hanceville will overwhelm a person with the grace of what is beautiful.

The Grace of Faithfulness to Death

Holy Family Parish—Shrine and Museum of Blessed Miguel Pro

Mexico City, Mexico

In the early 1900s, Catholic believers in Mexico faced persecution. It was during the time of the Cristero War in Mexico that many martyrs for the faith were given to the Church. One priest, Fr. Miguel Pro, was a Jesuit who did not give up his ministry of celebrating Mass and preaching the gospel. In 1927, there was an attempted assassination of a military general which prompted his arrest. While he was not responsible for the crime, the state viewed him as a threat. Fr. Miguel Pro did not back down and on November 23, 1927, he stood before a firing squad, proclaimed loudly and boldly, "Viva Cristo Rey," and clinging to a rosary and crucifix, died that day.

The Catholic Church in the United States has many Spanish-speaking Catholics. I was introduced to Blessed Miguel Pro during my time in the seminary. The renovation of the theology student chapel at Mundelein Seminary saw the installation of a stained glass window of Blessed Miguel Pro. He was a priest who remained faithful to the end. His story was meant to inspire us in our studies and ministry.

While visiting Mexico City, a city where a shrine to Blessed Miguel Pro was, it made sense to visit. I arrived at Holy Family Parish in Mexico City by Uber. I entered the church and noticed the image and relics of Miguel Pro to the right of the sanctuary. I prayed in the church in the presence of the saint whose relics were there. I prayed for my priesthood, asking that in times of persecution I would remain faithful to the end like Blessed Miguel Pro. We do not know what will become of the Christian faith in years to come. The message preached by Christianity is antithetical to the world. The world is threatened by the message and teaching of Jesus, and as in the past, could seek to obliterate it. We must be prepared and ready should that ever happen.

When the Church celebrates a memorial of a martyr, I'll typically choose Faith of Our Fathers as the closing song for Mass. The words of verse one say:

Faith of our fathers, living still
In spite of dungeon, fire and sword,
O how our hearts beat high with joy
Whene'er we hear that glorious word!
Faith of our fathers! Holy faith!
We will be true to thee till death!

It is a moving thought to think of our forefathers in the faith. There have been martyrs from the very beginning—John the Baptist, the apostles, and down through the centuries to this day. The story of the martyrs always encourages me to want to be true to the Lord until death. When I think of Blessed Miguel Pro, that is what I hope my grace will be, that I might die remaining faithful to the Lord. That no matter what happens, I will never give up believing in the Lord.

Parishioners of and visitors to Holy Family Parish in Mexico City have the reminder of a holy man, a blessed, hopefully soon a saint, who remained faithful through trials and tests, never renouncing his faith. He chose to die rather than to deny the Lord. If you have the chance to pray before the relics of Blessed Miguel Pro, I suggest praying to remain faithful to the end like he did.

The Grace of Availability

Holy Rood Catholic Church

Watford, England

Daily Mass is important to me as a priest. When I travel on vacation, I celebrate Mass daily. When I'm away from the parish it means that I have open Mass intentions on those occasions and can offer Mass for deceased loved ones and other intentions. When I travel, I do so with a travel Mass kit. It has a smaller chalice, a container that holds the celebrant hosts, and a paten on which to place the bread to be consecrated. The travel kit is convenient to say Mass in a hotel room or Air BnB. It's preferable if, when traveling, I can arrange to say Mass at a shrine or local parish. It is more dignified and meaningful. Sometimes, due to time constraints, that doesn't happen.

While visiting England with another priest, we found ourselves in the town of Watford. The church we'd wanted to celebrate Mass that day wasn't available, so one option was to celebrate Mass at the house where we were staying. It was the feast of the Triumph of the Holy Cross, and being a feast day or solemnity, my friend wasn't pleased with the idea of a low Mass at the house and wanted to find a church. We found the parish church in Watford and contacted the pastor, Fr. Gerard. We explained our situation and Fr. Gerard made the church available for us to celebrate Mass.

Fr. Gerard adjusted his schedule to welcome us and set up for Mass. It was fitting for us to say Mass at this church on this special day, because Holy Rood is the English equivalent of Holy Cross. We were going to celebrate Mass in a church on its patronal feast. As Catholics, relics are important to us, and to me. I hoped to venerate a relic of the true cross on this special feast day. Fr. Gerard, without skipping a beat, offered us the opportunity before I could even ask.

My priest friend and I offered Mass on a side altar in the Church. Nearby were plaques and reminders to pray for souls who made possible the construction of the church. One man even perished during its construction. I had them in mind as we celebrated that Mass. I'm not sure how many people fill that church for an ordinary Sunday, but they truly are blessed by the pastor they had in Fr. Gerard. His openness, hospitality, and kindness spoke volumes to me. It was a reminder too, that as a pastor, I would hope if an itinerant priest came calling at our parish or knocking on the door for a place to say Mass, that I would graciously be available to Him so that he could do the most important thing he could do that day, offer the Holy Sacrifice of the Mass.

Holy Rood Church was open for parishioners passing by to stop and pray. I'm sure as one older gentleman walked in, he wondered why two priests were at the side altar celebrating Mass. Most likely you will never have the opportunity or reason to visit Holy Rood Catholic Church. But what I learned from that visit offers a much wider opportunity for us. If your parish church is open during the day, consider yourself blessed. It's great that the church is open, but what's even better is that the Blessed Sacrament is readily available. You can come and pray before the Lord who waits in the tabernacle for you. Jesus makes himself available to you, so that you can be available to Him, and from there, accomplish His will in the world.

The Grace of Saintly Witness

The Cathedral of St. Cloud

St. Cloud, Minnesota

How many cities can you name with saint names? Saint Paul or St. Louis might come to mind. If you are quick with languages, you'll know that San Francisco or San Antonio are Spanish for St. Francis and St. Anthony. Saint names of cities speaks to the great influence Catholicism has had on different regions of our country. There is an obscure saint city in Minnesota, St. Cloud, and when I happened to visit the area, I wondered if St. Cloud was even a real person. It turns out he was.

St. Cloud was named as such not because of missionaries who christened the village but because of the Paris suburb where Napoleon had his favorite palace. It doesn't seem that St. Cloud the saint had any influence on the naming of the city. As the Catholic Church divided into dioceses throughout states, the Catholic Diocese of St. Cloud was established in 1889, taking none other than St. Cloud as its patron.

When I visit the seat of a diocese or archdiocese, if I am able, I like to visit the cathedral. It is the principal church of the local Catholic community and often breathtakingly beautiful. During a visit to the St. Cloud area, I decided to visit their cathedral. While I knew the city had the name of saint, I didn't know Cloud was a person. I entered the cathedral as I would any other cathedral, shrine, or church. I had no prior knowledge about the building. I was entering blindly not knowing what I would find. I was surprised to discover a shrine to St. Cloud. It was a simple altar, tucked away on the side. I wondered if people have a devotion to St. Cloud and for what they might ask his intercession. He was there in priestly vestments holding a chalice or ciborium communicating to me his eucharistic devotion. I also found a pamphlet with a biography about him. I was amazed at what I read about his life. and made a mental note that St. Cloud would be the subject of my homily on All Saints Day. Why? He surrounded himself with holy people.

St. Cloud was born in 522. After his parents died, he was entrusted to the care of his grandparents King Clovis and St. Clotilde. After his father's death, a jealous uncle wanted to take control of the throne and plotted Cloud's and his brother's deaths. . His brothers were murdered but Cloud survived. He sought refuge from St. Remigius, a bishop, and later came under the influence of the hermit St. Severin. Cloud didn't necessarily choose a life of silence and solitude, it was chosen for him by his uncle who forced him into hiding, but Cloud embraced that life, becoming holy, and even a saint.

In his life, St. Cloud had three saintly role models who formed him and cared for him. Reading his biography made me realize that we all need saintly people in our lives. Holy people attract other holy people. The family members of St. Therese were holy witnesses surrounding each other with their love for God. What about your friends? Are they leading you closer to God? Do they help you live a virtuous life? Are your friends helping you become a saint? As I prayed seeking the intercession of St. Cloud, I asked him for the grace to have saintly people around me. Praying for that grace meant I needed to examine my friendships and re-evaluate those relationships. St. Cloud, the person, gave me a deeper desire to be surrounded by holy men and women. Not only did I need to examine my friendships, but I had to examine my own contributions to friendships. Was I exuding holiness? Was I leading people to be saints? In my life, I've had friends challenge me to holiness. Once when I was saying unkind things about a person, someone walked away from the conversation. It spoke volumes to me and the thought has remained with me ever since. If I want to become a saint, then I need saintly influencers around me. I have St. Cloud to thank for this grace.

FIVE

GRAVES OF HOLY MEN & WOMEN

The Grace of Conviction

Grave of Irving "Francis" Houle

Escanaba, Michigan

When I was a teenager, a group from my parish would drive from Oconto, Wisconsin to Escanaba, Michigan. We would spend the day at an individual's home, praying with an elderly gentleman, and being prayed over by him. They called the man Francis, but his given name was Irving Houle. He was dubbed Francis because, like St. Francis of Assisi, this gentleman had the stigmata, that is the nail marks of Jesus, in his hand. Other famous saintly stigmatists include St. (Padre) Pio of Pietrelcina, St. Rita, and St. Catherine of Siena.

People drew near to Francis. They regarded him as a holy man because of the stigmata. They would ask him to pray for specific intentions and he would lay his hands on the person's head and offer a prayer from the heart for them. I'm certain people received answers to the prayers he offered for them. Francis would travel to parishes and offer witness talks and prayed over people. I don't remember how many times I visited Escanaba, but I know it was more than once. When news of Francis's death was disseminated, I attended his funeral Mass.

While I'm sure Francis wouldn't have known my name, maybe he would have recognized me. I felt a special closeness to him. During my formable teenage years, meeting a man with the stigmata, convicts your heart about belief in God. Chatrooms were big when I was a kid. They were on Yahoo or some other platform. Ministries had chatrooms or message boards. I ventured onto a Christian chatroom once led by a ministry promoted on the local Christian radio station. I remember logging in and asking one of their evangelical mentors if it was okay that I believed in God because of this man with the stigmata. I'm sure the person on the other end didn't know what to make of it. These signs and wonders of our faith though are encouragement to us. A man having the wounds of Jesus and then having them disappear after his death confounds the scientific mind. The stories of Francis's agony that he experienced during Holy Week were striking and made me think I needed to change my life and love God more.

Since his death, interest in Irving Francis Houle has increased. The Diocese of Marquette has begun the process to investigate whether or not Francis could be declared a saint, hopefully some day after the saintly bishop who served in Marquette, Frederic Baraga.

On one summer afternoon, I decided to make the drive to Escanaba. I knew the priest who served the parishes there. I asked him if he wanted to get lunch. He obliged. We had a great time of priestly fraternity and supporting each other as brother priests. The purpose of my visit was that I wanted to pray at the grave of Francis. Father already had an idea of where Francis could be interred in his home parish should his cause advance.

As I knelt at the grave for a moment of prayer, I asked Francis to intercede for my faith. That I could have the faith of a child who was moved to love God more on account of what God accomplished in Francis's life. Knowing Francis and having him pray over me strengthened my faith. I hoped that experience at his grave would have a similar effect as it did on me when I was a youth. I think it did.

The Grace of Introduction

Tomb of Venerable Maria Kaupas

Sisters of St. Casimir Motherhouse, Chicago, Illinois

Fr. Samuel Russell, O.S.B., was the rector of Conception Seminary College during my two years there. The first year I was intimidated by him as an authority figure. My second and final year I began to look to him as a father figure, especially as a spiritual father. During the seminarian's senior year, Fr. Samuel would take them to St. Louis and Chicago on a tour of two major seminaries—Kenrick and Mundelein. In St. Louis, he also took us to the beautiful Cathedral Basilica, a must see. Fr. Samuel was from Chicago so the visit to Mundelein and Chicagoland was an opportunity for him to share his life with us. He took us to visit his childhood parish and numerous other sites. One of these places was to the motherhouse for the Sisters of St. Casimir. The sisters were located in his neighborhood, and he had a lifelong friendship with them.

I remember when we were at Kenrick, the seminary was going to have an extraordinary form Mass that morning. Concelebration with another priest is not possible in the extraordinary form and Fr. Samuel wished to celebrate a Mass himself. That's what priests do. The celebration of Mass is central to our life, identity, and mission. It happened to be March 4, the feast of St. Casimir. I distinctly remember Fr. Samuel saying it was important for him to celebrate the Mass for the intentions of the sisters of St. Casimir as he had promised them.

It would only be a few days after that Mass I attended with Fr. Samuel for the Sisters of St. Casimir, that I would be introduced to them, their motherhouse, and their foundress. The memory of the Sisters of St. Casimir and Mother Maria stayed with me long after that senior class trip. When the sisters were telling us their story, they gave us literature about their community. I was tasked with bringing back all the materials to the seminary and after distribution, the leftovers remained in my possession for many years. Since that visit in 2011, what was ingrained in my Catholic memory and consciousness about the experience, was that Mother Maria Kaupas was buried in the back corner of their chapel in a sarcophagus. It was probably the first time I saw something of that sort. I am certain that I prayed in front of the tomb. For what, I don't know. It was a moment of prayer, asking another holy person on the road to sainthood to pray for me and my vocation.

I went to Mundelein Seminary in the Chicagoland area. I always recalled that visit to Mother Kaupas's tomb and her presence in that chapel. During my four years at Mundelein, I never made it back to the sisters to pray before the someday saint's tomb. I longed to but life is filled with good intentions. In 2024, I had the chance to return. I was intentional about it. Looking at the calendar, an upcoming Monday, my day off, was March 4, the feast of St. Casimir. I thought how appropriate to return. I called the sisters and inquired if I could pray at the tomb of Mother Kaupas. I could, and so I did.

Fr. Samuel Russell had passed away on November 14, 2023. As I returned to that chapel to pray before the tomb of the foundress of a religious community that was dear to him, I had him in mind as I prayed, thanking God for his priesthood, monastic life, and his spiritual fatherhood. Returning to that special devotional area, it was as I had remembered it, but it was new again to me. I knelt on the kneeler, prayed the prayers they had on display, and glanced at the petition book. I recognized a name from the book, and wondered if it would have been the person I met several years ago at a Catholic event. At the very least, if it was not him, I was reminded of that person and the kindness he showed me and remembered him in prayer to this saintly woman.

I was introduced to Venerable Mother Maria Kaupas because of Fr. Samuel Russell, O.S.B. If he never would have taken us to the motherhouse, I would have lived my Catholic life most likely without knowing about her unless she one day is declared Blessed or Saint. Because I know her, I can be inspired by her story, which is now told at the motherhouse in a special legacy museum. In addition to learning about Mother's life and the mission of the order, the bedroom of Mother Kaupas has been reconstructed in the area. The sayings of this holy woman can stay with me and be a source of inspiration. Her prayers can help me. This is the grace of introduction. I am willing to bet that at some point in your spiritual life, you have been introduced to a spiritual writer, priest, or religious, and that introduction has made a big difference in your life. While knowing who Mother Kaupas is and praying at her grave hasn't been life changing, I know it makes a spiritual difference for me. My whole priesthood has been spent introducing people to obscure holy people that I've encountered (see my book: How They Love Mary) and to holy sites. Without Fr. Samuel, you wouldn't know about Mother Kaupas, and would not know you could visit her in Chicago. If you ever find yourself in the little Lithuanian community of Chicago, stopping by her grave and saying a prayer might be worth it, because in so doing, you too will meet Mother Kaupas.

The Grace of Preaching and Evangelization

Tomb of Venerable Fulton Sheen

St. Mary's Cathedral, Peoria, Illinois

Archbishop Fulton Sheen was a notable figure of American Catholicism. Most people could recognize him from a photo or by his voice from his radio and television show. His content is still relevant and played on Catholic television and radio. Apps contain talks and homilies he gave. For years I tried to read Fulton Sheen's writings but never was able to finish a book. They were good, don't get me wrong, but I guess I didn't appreciate him. That changed when I read his autobiography Treasure in Clay. Getting to know him and his story helped me to appreciate and finish some of his other books I had struggled to read.

During some travels through the state of Illinois to St. Louis, I would often pass by El Paso, Illinois, which happens to be the city where Fulton Sheen was baptized. I stopped to visit and pray at the church once. Another time, I took a group of high school students there to emphasize the importance of baptism, knowing who baptized you, where you were baptized, and who your godparents are. Sheen was ordained a priest for the Diocese of Peoria. For years, he was entombed at St. Patrick's Cathedral in New York City. After a lengthy legal battle, Sheen's body was sent home to Peoria's Cathedral where his tomb is visited by devotees and followers.

Fulton Sheen has been inspiration to many priests because of his book The Priest is Not His Own. Sheen's spirituality has influenced countless priests and seminarians. His witness to the value of a daily holy hour is encouragement for every priest to spend time praying before the Blessed Sacrament every day. His love for Our Lady was evident because he pledged to celebrate a Mass in her honor every Saturday. He called her The World's First Love and visited many of her shrines throughout the world.

His television show Life is Worth Living was watched by millions and earned him an Emmy. His words, teaching, and preaching transcend time and are just as relevant today as they were during his time. As I prayed at his tomb, I thanked God for the life and vocation of Fulton Sheen. I prayed that I could preach like he did and reach people like him too. I have been involved in media apostolates like EWTN and Relevant Radio. I'm a podcaster and seek to communicate the gospel through media like Fulton Sheen. I prayed for him to inspire my work in that regard. As an author, I thought of his many publications and works, and placed a few of them on his tomb during my prayer.

I have looked to this holy communicator of the gospel to inspire and intercede for me. His life and work drew me to pray at his tomb. The work he did is continued by another generation. As one who has completed the race, he intercedes now for the Church he loved and served.

The Grace of Appreciation

Grave of Blessed James Miller

St. Martin Cemetery, Custer, Wisconsin

In the Catholic world, people might be familiar with author and speaker Meg Hunter Kilmer. Her claim to fame was living as a hobo for Christ. Essentially, she was homeless, owned a car, went around speaking from parish to parish, couch surfing to proclaim the gospel. She's written some great books about the saints. She has a fascination with lesser-known and diverse saints. One day on social media, I noticed that she was in Wisconsin. I lived about an hour away from where she was so I messaged her and said if she was free, I would love to catch dinner with her and bounce some ideas off her and get her feedback. It ended up being a fruitful conversation because she gave me a few names for my book, *How They Love Mary*. One of the people ended up becoming a person that deeply impacted me. I tried to visit the grave of that nun, but due to COVID precautions the nuns were uncomfortable with me visiting.

Meg was in Wisconsin to speak about the saints at a parish. In her, I have a kindred spirit, because she was willing to drive out of her way to visit the grave of Blessed James Miller. He was buried in a small, rural cemetery near Stevens Point, Wisconsin. As we had dinner, she shared a little bit about life of Blessed James, with whom I was unfamiliar. I heard his name, because the Daughters of St. Paul book In Caelo et in Terra had a sketch of him for one of the days of the 365-day book. Meg shared with me her dismay at what she found. The church near the cemetery, which no longer operated as a church, was now a storage building in disrepair. She also was dumbfounded that here you have a blessed, a person who has been beatified by the church, buried in a simple parish cemetery instead of a church or more prominent location. She thought, why not make the closed church a shrine to Blessed Miller.

One day, I happened to be driving to Stevens Point. I saw the cemetery, and recognized it as the cemetery where Blessed James Miller was buried. I didn't know how I would find his grave, but the cemetery was not that large, so I looked, and the website Find a Grave was of great help. I had no connection to him except living in the same state as him. I found the grave which indicated that he belonged to the Christian Brothers and was a missionary to Guatemala. I found it odd that Blessed James Miller was buried in the parish cemetery, in the family plot, and not with his conferees in a cemetery connected to the Christian Brothers, like the one in Winona, Minnesota. I can't say that I had a profound experience at the grave. I prayed my breviary, thinking that I was praying the same prayers that Blessed James had prayed in his life. After taking a picture and recording a video for social media, I got in my car and carried on with my travels, grateful for the brief moment of prayer and remembrance of a holy man.

If I had to identify a grace that I received at his grave, I would say it is the grace of appreciation. As a Catholic, living in Wisconsin, I appreciated who he was, who God called him to be, and how he responded to that call. He lived a simple and holy life. It's what we all are supposed to do. He's a member of the communion of the Saints with his cause on the road to sainthood. I appreciate his prayers of intercession and his saintly witness. We don't have to feel as strong of a connection to all the saints. But I think the best we can do, is at least appreciate them. One way to do that is by thanking God for their life, their witness, and their intercession.

A Grace Against Mediocrity

The Grave of Servant of God Frederic Baraga

St. Peter's Cathedral, Marquette, Michigan

My history of knowing about Bishop Frederic Baraga dates back many years. In my early days of visiting the National Shrine of Our Lady of Champion, the gift store owners had a fondness for the story of Bishop Baraga. The Catholic world in the Midwest can be quite small. If you are involved and invested in one Catholic project, you might be interested and invested in other Catholic projects too. If you love Marian shrines, you might like someday saints like Bishop Baraga. The gift store promoted material about Bishop Baraga. I remember the beige shirts with the portrait of Baraga on it that were available—a way to promote and spread his name and make him better known. I'm not sure it has worked. I also had checked out a book from the Green Bay Public Library. The red-covered book was the missionary journal of Bishop Baraga. It was in the beginning days of my Marian research. I wanted to read the diary to see if he referenced Our Lady. I'm not sure I ever finished the journal. What I do remember, the hefty late fee for not returning the book by its due date.

I had heard Baraga's name off and on but didn't really do much to learn more about him or develop a devotion to him. Another Green Bay priest and I have visited several graves for future saints. We were scheming one day, and I mentioned how I would love to go and pray at his grave. It just seemed like the right Catholic and priestly thing to do. We scheduled our pilgrimage to the Upper Peninsula of Michigan for the first week of January. Who does that? They had snow, and during our commute, there were light flurries. We arrived safely in Marquette and looked forward to visiting the cathedral where Baraga was buried the next morning. We were scheduled to concelebrate at Mass and would pray privately in the Church after Mass. It was a delightful visit.

Bishop Baraga was born in 1797. He came to the United States in 1830 as a priest, was consecrated a bishop in 1853, and served the Church until his death in 1868. Baraga took his ministry seriously. One could not accuse him of being lazy. His ministry focused on the Native Americans. He set out to learn their language. He wrote down the Chippewa language in a dictionary and evangelized the Natives in their own language. He also traversed the wintery wonderland of the Upper Peninsula by snowshoe to visit churches to celebrate the sacraments and preach the gospel.

If there was one thing I prayed for as I knelt before his tomb in a side chapel of the cathedral, it was for the grace against mediocrity and apathy. I'll admit, some days I hope for a snow day like a school kid. Sometimes you just want a day to catch up without everything else happening. As I reflected and prayed about the life of Bishop Baraga, I realized he would never pray for a snow day, and if there was snow, he wouldn't let that stop him. I prayed to have the fervor and zeal of Bishop Baraga, to receive just a portion of his priestly spirit.

In addition to the cathedral, just down the road in Marquette, is the Bishop Baraga Association, headquartered in the rectory in which Bishop Baraga lived. It is worth a visit to see the museum and artifacts of the future saint, including a relic that facilitated a healing on the day of his funeral. Roughly an hour-and-a-half from Marquette is the city of L'Anse, a city that was central to the ministry of Bishop Baraga. A sixty-foot statue of Baraga graces the property and might be of interest to devotees. Students of American history and disciples of Catholicism find in Bishop Baraga an interesting figure of history and Catholicism. A Slovenian missionary to the Native Americans, he gained converts, and preached the gospel. He's an inspiration most certainly to priests, but his life and story has something for everybody. Let his witness be one of taking a stand against mediocrity.

The Grace of Renewal

The Grave of Venerable Samuel Mazzuchelli, OP

St. Patrick's Parish Cemetery, Benton, Wisconsin

You know certain things or are aware of certain people when you are immersed in the Catholic world. Because I live in Wisconsin and serve in the Diocese of Green Bay, I had an awareness of the Venerable Fr. Samuel Mazzuchelli. He was an early Dominican missionary to Wisconsin, founded an order of religious sisters (Sinsanawa Dominicans), and ministered in the Diocese of Green Bay. He formed the parish community of St. John the Evangelist in downtown Green Bay and oversaw the construction of its first church. I recall a seminarian had a book about Mazzuchhelli, it seemed to be more of a doctoral dissertation because of its profundity and depth. I don't think he read it, but he did loan it to a priest who was interested.

In conversation with a brother priest at a clergy gathering, he shared with me his interest in making a pilgrimage to the grave of Fr. Samuel Mazzuchelli. I told him I would be interested. We planned on a date and we made it happen. Unfortunately, it had to be a quick trip. Basically, we drove three hours, arrived, had an hour there, and had to leave right away because I needed to get back for an evening commitment. Even though the visit was rushed, it was a blessing to me at that time.

Considering that this is a travel memoir, it behooves me as the author to be frank and honest. My visit to the grave of Samuel Mazzuchelli came at a time when I was at a low in my life and ministry. I needed a little pick-me-up that would encourage me and incite a greater zeal for souls. I needed priestly renewal. The priest with whom I traveled heard my confession at the grave, and together we prayed our Daytime Prayer and the prayer for his beatification. I thought about Fr. Samuel, and his own life of ministry and how he served the people of Benton, Wisconsin.

He was their parish priest. He knew them. He prayed with them and for them. He preached the gospel to them. He heard their confessions. I experienced a profound renewal at the grave of Fr. Mazzuchelli. It felt as if he was giving me his priestly spirit. I'm not lying. I journaled about it and was amazed by the impact that simple visit to his grave had on me.

While in Benton, we admired the small rectory that served as the home for the simple Dominican pastor. He lived humbly. My priest friend and I stopped in Schullsburg at a church established by Mazzuchelli. He named the streets in the community after virtues and other theological themes like judgement and friendship. Young men from the Diocese of Green Bay who are beginning their formation as priests and also those discerning a vocation now make a visit to Mazzuchelli's grave in Benton. They even walk in Mazzuchelli's footsteps, making the trek as a walking pilgrimage, traveling on foot to visit places significant to Mazzuchelli in Dubuque and the Diocese of Madison. I hope that as they learn his story and pray at his grave, that he will give them that same fervor and spirit that I received. As they pray and discern, I hope renewal will be theirs, just as it was mine.

SIX

MONASTERIES

The Grace of Stability

Conception Abbey

Conception, Missouri

Conception Abbey is a Benedictine monastery in rural Northwest Missouri. They also have a college seminary where young men earn their BA in philosophy while being formed for the priesthood. The Benedictine life follows the Rule of St. Benedict who is considered the founder of western monasticism. Monks gather for prayer several times a day, either five or seven times. They chant what is called the Divine Office, known to many as the Liturgy of the Hours. The Divine Office is comprised of Psalms and canticles, and besides the Eucharist, it is the foundation of the spiritual life of a monastery. In addition to the evangelical counsels (or vows) of chastity, poverty, and obedience, the Benedictines also vow themselves to stability. This means that they will spend their life at the monastery with few exceptions of external assignments.

The monks of Conception Abbey arrived in the 1870s and were led by Abbot Frowin Conrad. The monastery of Engelberg Abbey in Einsiedeln, Switzerland supplied the founding members. Men from throughout the United States have joined Conception Abbey. Some remain as brothers for the entirety of their monastic life, while some brothers are called to serve as priests for the sacramental and spiritual needs of the community. A few miles down the road from the abbey today is a community of Benedictine religious sisters, whose spiritual needs are provided by the monks of Conception Abbey. One monk, who has a cause for canonization, Fr. Lukas Etlin, OSB, served as their chaplain for many years until his death in 1927.

When I was an undergraduate student, I took courses through three different colleges/universities before arriving at Conception Seminary College. I went to the seminary right out of high school and attended a university and seminary in Minnesota. Then I went to St. Norbert College for a year. Admittedly, I was not able to afford the spring semester, so I joined the workforce. When I decided to enter the seminary, I wanted to stay on track to graduate in four years, and had the funds to take some online classes through St. Leo University in Florida. From 2007 to 2009, my life was anything but stable. There were constant moves from college to college and uncertainty about what I was doing or where I was going. I found the stability that the monastery and their seminary offered comforting for me. I entered into the rhythm of prayer and formation and found a lot of peace in my two years on the grounds of Conception Abbey. I remember one day during my first year at Mundelein Seminary missing the life that Conception Abbey offered me. If I'm honest, I still yearn for it a bit today. I have not returned as often as I thought I would, but when the time is right, I know that Conception Abbey will be there for me.

All believers, regardless of denomination, can visit Conception Abbey. They have a guesthouse that offers retreats throughout the year. Their liturgies of the Divine Office and Eucharist are open to the public. If you are searching for something in your spiritual life, a retreat or getaway to a monastery like Conception Abbey might be what your soul needs.

The Grace of Rest

New Mellery Abbey

Peosta, Iowa

To get to Conception Abbey in Missouri from Northeast Wisconsin, the best route is through Iowa, crossing over into Dubuque. I'm not sure when I first learned about the Trappist monks at New Mellery Abbey, but I became more familiar with them during those trips. I made a fellow seminarian who traveled with me stop there. It was a convenient stop to use the bathroom and make a visit to the abbey church and pray privately for a few minutes. They also had a nice gift shop at which I bought a few Christmas presents for my family.

The Trappists at New Mellery have an interesting apostolate. They plant trees, maintain them, harvest them, and then craft caskets out of them. The idea of a monastic life is to be self-sufficient. People buying the caskets support the life of the monks. I recently had a funeral where the person was buried in one of those caskets. For most people attending the funeral, it was the first time they saw a simple monastic casket. Many priests, myself included, hope to be buried in a Trappist casket.

After graduating from Conception, those visits to New Mellery stopped for a long time. When I attended an ordination in the Archdiocese of Dubuque, I swung by the monastery as a way to "waste time" in a holy way. The visit did not disappoint and I actually crossed paths with a bishop I knew who was making a private retreat at the monastery. I know of another priest who frequents the abbey at least on an annual basis for his retreat. While I have never made a retreat there, I hope maybe one day I will.

The Abbey was a place where I could get out of the car and stretch my legs. It provided a rest from driving. But as an abbey, it offers much more than that. People who wish to escape from the world and rest with the Lord, visit, and stay at their retreat center. Their way of life and prayer invite us to take a break from the world and enter into their life of prayer. The Lord invites us to rest with him and lay our cares on Him. This can take place at the abbey or in another holy setting. And it actually happens each week, as the Lord invites us to enter into sabbath rest on the day of the Lord. Let us ask the Lord to give us this grace to receive the gift of holy rest.

The Grace of Ruins
Mellifont Abbey
Ireland

I had the chance to take a course in monastic history during my years at Conception Seminary College. The professor I had for the class, Brother Thomas, ended up being one of my favorite professors in my journey of higher education. During my time at Conception Seminary, I enrolled in as many classes as I could with Brother Thomas. Little facts from his classes remain still today in my bank of knowledge.

It was in the fall of 2010 that I noticed the Mariological Society of America would have as its theme, "Mary in the United States and Canada up to 1900." I knew that it would be a chance to research and write about the Wisconsin apparition in Champion witnessed by Adele Brise. I submitted my paper proposal, and when the MSA accepted it, I turned to Brother Thomas for guidance. My final semester at Conception Seminary, 2011, under his tutelage, I undertook what would begin my "career" in the discipline of Mariology, using research to craft a presentation to give at a major academic conference. I was elected to the MSA Administrative Council in 2016, its vice president in 2020, and its president in 2022. I have Brother Thomas to thank for his influence.

When I visited Ireland for the first—and hopefully not the last—time, I knew I wanted to visit the ruins of Mellifont Abbey because my research paper for my monastic history class focused on this abbey. Mellifont was a Cistercian abbey in Ireland, founded in 1142. The abbey held a great influence in Catholic medieval Ireland and led to the establishment of more than 35 daughter houses throughout Ireland. The monastery stood strong until it was surrendered to the Crown on June 23, 1538.

As you drive through Ireland, you will happen upon signs for ruins of monasteries, much like the brown informational signs we have come to know in the United States. While that is a sad state of affairs in and of itself, the ruins speak to the presence of prayer and dedication of monks long ago. Mellifont Abbey was not the only site of ruins my priest friend and I visited during our pilgrimage there. One day we had no place scheduled to celebrate Mass and since I traveled with my Mass kit, we decided to pray Mass at one of the ruins, Corcomroe Abbey, atop what we believed was the altar from centuries ago. Across the street from Crough Patrick, was Murrisk Friary. Being two priests, we were inclined to explore the ruins. It was time for Vespers, or evening prayer, of the Liturgy of the Hours, and so in a place where friars long ago prayed and sang the divine office, we did the same. When it came time to pray the Our Father, we chanted it in Latin, knowing that would have been the language in which our ancestors in the faith would have prayed and chanted.

My visit to Mellifont Abbey might have been anti-climactic but I wanted to go just to see the place that I had studied and read about. I was able to find my research paper, re-read it, and bring it with me to the ruins. Part of the paper analyzed the layout of the monastery. Just as monks would have roamed those halls, I wandered the ruins. One could close their eyes, and just imagine what life in this monastery would have been like. Walking and praying on those grounds, and other monastic ruins in Ireland, made me realize that as Catholic Christians, we stand on the shoulders of those who have gone before us in the faith. Their life was a witness to belief in God, lived out through prayer and vocation. The grace of ruins reminds us of our past and to appreciate what once was. As one happens upon ruins of monasteries in Ireland, in the United States we come across closed churches and suppressed religious communities. We are reminded of history and people's contributions to Catholicism, all of which should move us to thank God for what has been and to pray for what will be.

The Grace of Oblation

Corpus Christi Monastery

Poor Clare Colettines, Rockford, Illinois

Before Facebook, Twitter (now X), and other social media sites were popular, communities were built online through online forums. From what I can tell, forums have faded into near non-existence, because Facebook groups and such took over. When I see #CatholicTwitter and the community it has, it makes me remember my high school days of being a part of a Catholic online forum. The forum kept track of how many posts you made, and you would creep up the tier and reach new levels. People on the forum could correspond with each other and they supported one another by prayer and in other ways too. Some members were Protestants, hoping to understand the Catholic faith, and some would end up converting to Catholicism. Some members married each other. How amazing to think that a Catholic online community would lead to love, marriage, and children. There was a special section called "The Vocation Station" where individuals who felt called to a vocation in the Church could share topics, converse, and support each other in their discernment. A thread was pinned to the top of members who ended up joining religious communities. Holy friendships were formed at the Vocation Station, and I correspond with a few religious sisters and one-time discerners today. Every now and again on Facebook, I will see a post and recall the person's username and look with interest to see where their life has led them.

One person I corresponded with on the forum joined the Poor Clare Colettines in Rockford, Illinois. They are a cloistered religious community meaning once a young woman joins, she will not go home to her family on a home visit or leave the monastery except for medical appointments. She will spend her left separated from the world, a barrier called a grille preventing human embrace. When I have shared about this life on social media, some people are turned off by it, and want to emancipate the nuns. What that person fails to realize is that those women have chosen this way of life. God has led them into the desert to pray and to be all His. God has given that person the grace to live this life of intimate union with God, praying and offering their life for the Church. It is said that the Church is sustained by the prayers of these cloistered religious who offer their lives in hiddenness.

I studied alongside other men for the priesthood from the Diocese of Rockford. One would become a close priest friend, who has since entered religious life after serving as a diocesan priest for several years. When I attended his diaconate ordination back in 2014, I stopped at the monastery where this young woman had entered. When I rang the bell, a sweet little old nun, who I now know is called an extern sister, answered on the intercom. Two other seminarians and I wanted to pray for a bit in their chapel. When I related this to the sister, she said, "Jesus would like that very much." A simple statement, but it's true. Jesus liked our visit very much. He likes any time that we choose to spend with him. This was my first visit to the monastery, and I admired a lot in the church. There was a stunning stained-glass window of Mary receiving Holy Communion from the hand of St. John. That image would be on my holy card commemorating my ordination as a priest and, from time to time, is the lock screen on my iPhone.

There was something special about praying in that church, knowing that my friend prays there several times a day and that she has dedicated her life to that house of prayer. I would return to the monastery in 2015 after my ordination to offer a Mass of Thanksgiving. Another visit would be for that young woman's perpetual profession as a nun. And recently, I attained a plenary indulgence by praying before the manger scene in a Franciscan church during the 800th anniversary of the first Christmas manger. One time, when I had a special intention that I needed serious prayer for, I wrote my sister friend and asked her to pray. She did and eventually the grace of an answered prayer was obtained. She asked one time for me to place an extra host on the paten at Mass, as a way to remember an intention of hers in prayer. I obliged.

The cloistered life that she and the other nuns live in that monastery, and that other cloistered orders live, like the Carmelites or Handmaids of the Precious Blood, is an oblation to Jesus, that is to say, their life is an offering to Jesus for the sake of the Church. That is the grace of the monastery. It is for us to realize that oblation to Jesus has obtained much for the world and the Church. The Lord is pleased by their life and sacrifice, and we should be grateful for their dedication and prayer.

The Grace of Continuity

Mepkin Abbey

Moncks Corner, South Carolina

With an interest in all things Catholic, when I was on vacation in Myrtle Beach, I searched out holy places to visit. Mepkin Abbey was one of those places. My familiarity with the abbey was limited. When I served as a Godly Counsel on EWTN's Morning Glory show, host Gloria Purvis would mention the abbey because she hailed from South Carolina. Another time, when I attended the Catholic Marketing Network event, I met August Turak, a Templeton Prize winner for his book Brother John. During my conversation with August, he mentioned Mepkin Abbey to me, especially his involvement with, inspiration from, and appreciation for the monks. When I discovered that the abbey was located within driving distance of Myrtle Beach (about two hours), I deemed it worthy of a visit. Having been immersed in the Benedictine life, I looked forward to a visit to this Trappist monastery.

When I arrived on the grounds, it was a beautiful drive down their driveway, with tree branches creating a picturesque scene. I had no idea what I should expect as I made my way onto the grounds. I followed the signs and eventually arrived at the Welcome Center and Gift Shop. I had arrived on time for the tour. For $5, you received a booklet about Mepkin Abbey, and a tour with a guide to the monastery. During my visit, it was the head monk of the abbey. Typically, he would be called an abbot, but because of the numbers in the monastery, and that he served many years in leadership, he was not eligible to serve as abbot, though he functioned for all intents and purposes as one. He shared the history of the Trappist order, being a reform of the Benedictines and the Cistercians, and how the monastery of La Trappe was formed. He also shared about Mepkin Abbey, founded in 1949 as a daughter house of Gethsemani Abbey.

I was surprised by my visit to Mepkin Abbey, specifically that you only had access to the church if you arrived in time for the tour. Many of the monasteries I have visited, I did so without a designated time of arrival. I would plan to arrive for morning prayer, evening prayer, or compline, and pray the Divine Office with the monks. But, as part of this tour, guests were able to participate in the liturgical life of the monks by praying Daytime Prayer. Only retreatants had access to the monastery. If you plan to stop by Mepkin Abbey, be sure to visit their website, and find out what time you will need to arrive by in order to have the full experience.

After the tour, I arrived back at the gift store, and spoke with the people who worked there. After a casual conversation with one gentleman, he volunteered to give me a golf cart tour of the grounds and gardens during which he shared his own reflections on the monastery. One thing he said struck me. Since the foundation of the abbey in 1949, there has been a continuous prayer at the monastery. Even when natural disaster struck or a pandemic shut down the country, the monks still gathered to pray the Divine Office and offer the Holy Mass. There has been an unbroken succession of daily prayer. He encouraged me to think about all the graces that God has bestowed upon the monastery and the world because of their prayer. It made me think as a pastor that I could not say the same for the parishes I serve. There is no Mass on Monday when I take a day away from the parish. When I go on vacation for a week or we have a diocesan gathering, no Mass is offered then either.

After that golf cart ride, I had a greater appreciation for the monks of Mepkin Abbey. They have been a continuous place of prayer and worship where God continues to hear their prayers and pours out graces for them and all of us. For this, I give thanks, and hopefully you will too. Their witness encourages me to be pray without ceasing in my own life. It may not be at a monastery, but wherever I am, I can offer my prayers daily just as those monks do.

The Grace of a Thankful Heart

St. Leo Abbey

St. Leo, Florida

My Benedictine training fostered a love for the monastic life. My connection to St. Benedict predated Conception Seminary. The medal of St. Benedict is fairly popular as a sacramental. It is often worn to protect a person against attacks from the evil one. A St. Benedict medal came attached to my scapular. As I reflected previously, Conception Abbey provided me stability for two years after having taken classes through three different institutions before my arrival there. One of those places was St. Leo University. I didn't enroll there as a student in Florida. When I made the decision to withdraw from St. Norbert College, one day I received an email about St. Leo's College of Online Learning. I don't know how or why I received that email but it came at the precise right time. I contacted the admissions office and before I knew it, I was enrolled in some online classes. I appreciated the coursework, and recall enjoying the art history class I took.

I appreciated the coursework I was able to take through St. Leo University because it meant that I would stay on track to complete my college coursework in four years. In the journey toward the priesthood, it meant one less year I would spend in seminary and one more year of ministry in the Church. St. Leo University was an apostolate of St. Leo Abbey. My love for Benedictine life beckoned me to visit there. I knew one day I would but wasn't sure if it would be just as a day trip or for an extended stay at their retreat center. During one of my Florida trips, I made it a point to visit and pray there in thanksgiving for the gift their school gave me.

I knew monks prayed publicly the Liturgy of the Hours and planned my trip around Vespers. I emailed the Abbey to ensure that visitors were welcomed for prayer and shared that I planned on coming the following Wednesday. I received a correspondence back confirming I could attend Vespers. I arrived at St. Leo earlier than I expected and, as it would turn out, that was a blessing. I did what most people might do, I went to the monastery gift shop. I thought it would be nice to support their ministry and learn more about the abbey before visiting. I spoke with the kind brother who was working there and shared that I was a priest. By the time I checked out, I related my story of appreciation for St. Leo Abbey and University. I also inquired about the Abbey schedule. "Brother, Vespers is at 6:00 pm right?" "Not tonight," he said. I thought that odd since I had inquired the week before. He went on to share a text he received that stated Vespers was on their own that day and that their dinner reservation at a nearby restaurant was for 5:45 that evening. Apparently, this dinner escaped the monk who emailed me or came up suddenly. Who knew if the mysterious priest was actually going to show up or not.

It was about 4:00 p.m., without communal Vespers, I could pray my holy hour before the tabernacle and then take off much earlier than I anticipated. I opened the church doors and immediately the smell was familiar. It smelled like a monastic church. Probably the remnants of years of incense burning in the space, filling it with holy smoke and a fragrant aroma. As I walked in, I was struck by the paintings on the walls. Walking further into the church, along the perimeter were side altars dedicated to various saints both of the Benedictine tradition and other associated saints like St. Leo or St. Boniface. The first monk of St. Leo Abbey, Fr. Gerald Pilz, arrived in 1886 and was sent by Archabbot Boniface Wimmer of St. Vincent Archabbey in Latrobe, Pennsylvania. Fr. Gerald went to serve the German population, and St. Boniface was one of the evangelizers of Germany. The stained-glass windows flanking each altar represented one of the joyful or sorrowful mysteries. Special windows dedicated to St. Benedict and a statue of St. Benedict were in one devotional area, and there were the expected Joseph and Mary statues and corresponding stained-glass windows too.

The church was uniquely beautiful and a delight to spend time in praying. I sat down in a chair before the Blessed Sacrament and began my period of prayer. I didn't know what the relationship of students at the university to the Abbey looked like. From my walk on campus, it appeared they had a small, plain chapel, dedicated to the patron saint of hopeless causes, St. Jude. Two students came and sat down during my prayer time. I was impressed by their fervor and devotion. The one pulled out a prayer card of Blessed Carlo Acutis and prayed a prayer seeking his intercession or for his canonization. I was surprised when the church bells started ringing at 4:45. Another student entered the church and turned on all the lights. I leaned over and asked the gentleman in front of me, "What's going on?" He responded, "Mass is at 5:00." I was surprised by that. I didn't seem to recall that on the schedule, but I also wasn't looking for it. I wondered if it would be a conventual Mass for the Benedictines and students joined. I moved to the back of church so I could finish my meditation and then sneak off when Mass started. I thought to myself that it was a good thing I'd arrived early and prayed during the 4:00 hour because if I arrived to pray at 5:00 before 6:00 Vespers, I would have been doubly disappointed and would have had to find somewhere else to pray instead of the abbey church.

It all worked out. I prayed in the abbey church and saw the campus. I was impressed by the number of students who were attending daily Mass. And the answer to my wondering—the monks had Mass earlier in the day because it appeared to be the college's chaplain who was celebrating the Mass. I prayed in that church, grateful that a monk arrived in the 1880s and that the university was founded in 1889. One-hundred-and-twenty years after the university was founded, I would enroll as an online student to catch up on coursework to transfer into the seminary system. Without those monks and that university, it would have been one year less of hearing confessions and celebrating Mass. The year 2015 would have seen no ordinations for the Diocese of Green Bay. For St. Leo Abbey, I am grateful, and I was able to offer prayers of gratitude before the Blessed Sacrament, in a church that has echoed the praises of God for nearly 140 years.

CONCLUSION

Through videos I post online or having people join me on bus trips, I have had the opportunity to show so many holy places to people. Now through this book, I have been able to introduce you to places I have visited and shared with you the graces I received. Through this book and the short experiences at each shrine, chapel, monastery, or grave I visited, I hoped to communicate how important it is to appreciate the places we visit. My intention was not to provide a historical overview of the location or an analysis of its architecture. I'll leave that to you to figure out for the places you plan to visit. That's a part of the process for you and me to fall in love with a shrine or holy place. I need to learn, and as I learn, I begin to realize the impact it has on me as person and more importantly, as a believer.

The places I have written about, may not interest you, and that is okay. They are a part of my story as a believer and follower of Jesus. They impacted me, and if there is anything to take away from me sharing these visits, is to realize what can happen to you when you make similar visits. Our good God has something in store for you when you make time for Him at a holy place. There is a grace. You may know what it is immediately, or it might take you weeks, months, or even years to unpack and name it. You might even have to visit the place again and during the next visit the grace of God becomes more apparent. Some of these places I have visited numerous times, some I couldn't even give you a number of times I've been there (take for example the shrine in Champion, Wisconsin). There are others that I don't know if I would ever visit again, except if I'm nearby or want to show someone. But

God called me there that one time, for a reason and purpose, so that I could receive his grace for the present moment.

As I was writing this book, I hoped to get on a late afternoon Sunday flight in Milwaukee and fly to Oklahoma City. There is a new shrine to Blessed Stanley Rother that was constructed, dedicated, and now welcomes pilgrims. It's a beautiful church structure and seeing photos of it made me realize that beautiful churches can be built in the third millennium. When it was just a concept and they shared projected plans, I was moved to donate in support of the project. I hoped to include that visit in this travel memoir, but assuming there will be a volume two, I will have to write about it then. I intended to call it "The Grace of a Second Chance." I studied Spanish in Guatemala por ocho semanas (for eight weeks) at a Benedictine monastery in Quetzaltenango. I was aware of Blessed Stanley Rother and his ministry in Guatemala because a monk at Conception Abbey spent his summers in Oklahoma City helping promote his cause for sainthood. I had the opportunity to go to the village and church where Blessed Stanley was martyred, but I opted not to because I just wanted to rest and relax instead of keeping such a packed and fast-paced schedule. It is one of my bigger regrets to this day. I considered the shrine in Oklahoma City to offer me a second chance as there are relics of him there and I could ask the intercession of this heroic priest.

I'm already thinking about the rest of this year and next year. I know of places that I hope to visit. I'm hoping to visit Branson, Missouri and take in a show or two. During my visit, there are half a dozen places I want to visit, document, and share with my followers. Later this year, I'll be taking a bus group to Detroit to visit Blessed Solanus Casey's shrine and other Catholic sites. I will visit the Cross in the Woods for the first time and also the Basilica of St. Anne in Detroit. Through LinkedIn and my friendship with author James Hanna, I've become aware of the life of Bishop Broderick. I read the biography of this American prelate and was impressed by his life. When James Hanna took my suggestion of collecting the writings of Bishop Broderick, I graciously agreed to write the forward to the book. I hope to one day visit his grave in Hawthorne, New York. I've had the occasion to visit a grave of an ordinary priest, who I only knew through his Instagram posts. He lived in a city where I often vacation. I remarked to him that we should get dinner next time I was in town. Instead, I visited his grave. I have a good number of priest heroes, whose stories would only be brief in a book, but I hope to pay my respects and thank them for their priesthood while visiting their graves.

Shrines and chapels, monasteries, and graves, have taught me a lot about pursuing God, and have helped me feel connected to Our Lady, the saints, and the Church. I receive God's grace every day in the parish church in which I serve, pray, and celebrate Mass, and also at the holy sites I visit when I travel. They are places where I have received much grace, helping me on my pilgrimage to my Heavenly home. Until I arrive at those pearly gates, I remain here on earth with open hands, ready to receive the graces God gives me on the path to my heavenly destination.

ACKNOWLEDGEMENTS

Most of my writings have been published by traditional publishers. In self-publishing this book, I realized the value of having a team of people with a publisher. Everything that it takes to publish a book had to be led by my initiative. A manuscript needs to be edited and copyedited and proofread. Nancy Lind, Amanda Lauer, and Mary Ann Wagner helped in that process. Fr. Ian VanHeusen recommended a talented book designer who helped to shape the word document into a manuscript. Since I was publishing this book under a self-published imprint, Bon Secours Books, a logo was needed. I was able to hire one of my followers on X (formerly Twitter) to design it. A lot of people had to show patience toward me while I would share with them ideas or my progress with the manuscript. Thanks for your kindness, your words, and support. To my readers, followers, and parishioners, I can write in my free time because of you. If you did not read my books or follow my content, there would be no need for this book or any other book. Thanks for tagging along with me on my travel journeys but most especially through this journey of life and faith that we are on.

ABOUT THE AUTHOR

FR. EDWARD LOONEY was ordained a priest in 2015 for the Diocese of Green Bay. In addition to a Bachelor of Philosophy, a Baccalaureate in Sacred Theology (S.T.B.), and a Master of Divinity, he holds a Licentiate in Sacred Theology (S.T.L.) from the University of St. Mary of the Lake-Mundelein Seminary. Fr. Looney specializes in Marian theology, having authored numerous works on Mary, including *A Lenten Journey with Mother Mary* and *How They Love Mary: 28 Life-Changing Stories of Devotion to Our Lady* available from Sophia Institute Press.

He is a past president of the Mariological Society of America and continues to research, reflect, and write about Mary. Fr. Looney is a popular media personality, podcast host, and contributor to online publications and print publications like *Living Faith*. His interests include the Blessed Virgin, sainthood causes, shrines, and film/television.

OTHER BOOKS AVAILABLE FROM FR. EDWARD LOONEY

For Adults

A Heart Like Mary's
(Ave Maria Press)

A Rosary Litany
(Our Sunday Visitor)

Our Lady of Good Help: A Prayerbook for Pilgrims
(TAN Books)

A Lenten Journey with Mother Mary
(Sophia Institute Press)

Meditations After Holy Communion
(Sophia Institute Press)

Behold the Handmaid of the Lord
(Ave Maria Press)

How They Love Mary (Sophia Institute Press)

For Children

Fr. Looney's Christmas Stories
(Bon Secours Books)

The Story of Sister Adele
(Bon Secours Books)

Little Chapels, Grateful Hearts
(Bon Secours Books)

www.ingramcontent.com/pod-product-compliance
Lightning Source LLC
LaVergne TN
LVHW010625100826
845148LV00014B/3106

9798988403333